COMPUTERS:
PROCESSING
THE
DATA

INNOVATORS

INNOVATORS

COMPUTERS:
PROCESSING
THE
DATA

Gina De Angelis and David J. Bianco

The Oliver Press, Inc.
Minneapolis

The Oliver Press, Inc.
5707 West 36th Street
Minneapolis, MN 55416-2510

Library of Congress Cataloging-in-Publication Data
De Angelis, Gina.
    Computers: processing the data / Gina De Angelis and David J. Bianco.
       v. cm. — (Innovators ; v. 13)
    Includes bibliographical references and index.
    Contents: Charles Babbage and the analytical engine — Alan Turing and the Turing
Machine — John Mauchly and J. Presper Eckert and the electronic computer — Jack
Kilby and Robert Noyce and the integrated circuit — Marcian E. "Ted" Hoff and the
microprocessor — Steve Wozniak and the personal computer — Tim Berners-Lee and the
World Wide Web.
    ISBN 1-881508-87-0 (lib. bdg.)
    1. Computer science—History—Juvenile literature. 2. Computer
scientists—Biography—Juvenile literature. [1. Computer science—History. 2. Computer
scientists. 3. Scientists.] I. Bianco, David J., 1971- II. Title. III. Series.

QA76.17D43 2004
004'.09—dc22

                                                                2003064983

ISBN 1-881508-87-0
Printed in the United States of America
11 10 09 08 07 06 05   8 7 6 5 4 3 2 1

CONTENTS

From Clay Tokens to Calculating Machines

Numbers are old. Really old. Even before the dawn of recorded history, humans needed numbers to keep track of how much food they had, how much they could trade, and how much was still needed for the winter. And ever since then, people have spent a great deal of time coming up with devices to work with more and bigger numbers.

The first known use of a calculating device was to keep track of agricultural surpluses. As early as 2000 B.C., even before the people of the Middle East developed written numbers, they used small, fired-clay tokens to keep track of their produce. If one farmer gave another several bushels of wheat to store, he would receive in return an equal number of tokens that represented the bushels. Different types of produce required different types of tokens, so by examining the tokens in his possession, a farmer could determine how much and what kinds of produce he was owed.

Archaeologists believe humans first developed agriculture in about 8000 B.C. in the Fertile Crescent, located between the Tigris and Euphrates Rivers in ancient Assyria and Babylonia (present-day Iraq). The region's inhabitants later developed irrigation and domesticated food animals such as pigs and goats.

Before the development of calculating machines and computers, even the most complex mathematical problems had to be solved by hand-written calculations or with simple tools such as counting tokens.

Another early calculating device was the counting board. The first counting boards were nothing but sand held in shallow trays. A user made a series of parallel vertical lines in the sand, and the spaces between the marks corresponded to numbers—ones, tens, hundreds, and so on. By placing pebbles or other objects within the appropriate spaces, the user could keep count. Counting boards were well suited for use in outdoor marketplaces, and more affluent people owned wooden trays filled with sand that could also be used indoors.

The counting board was a precursor to one of the most recognizable of ancient counting devices: the abacus. The earliest example of an abacus appeared in China around A.D. 1200. Like most later abacuses, it featured a number of thin rods or wires strung with beads. A crossbar divided the rods into upper and lower sections. Each rod stood for a power of ten, so the rightmost rod represented ones, the second from the right represented tens, and so on. Adding a number required moving beads toward the crossbar, and subtracting involved moving beads away from it. Good abacus users could even multiply, divide, and take square or cube roots.

The abacus was speedy and popular, but it required training and practice to reach full proficiency, and there was an element of human error involved. The abacus did not actually do the computing—it simply helped the user keep track of the numbers, and dealing with large numbers or even many small ones could still get confusing. Over the years, inventors tried their hands at producing a better

solution. In around 1500, for instance, Leonardo da Vinci (1452-1519) sketched a design for a simple calculating machine that used interconnected wheels and gears. His drawings were incomplete, but working models have since been built from them.

In 1623, the German professor Wilhelm Schickard (1592-1635) produced the first functional mechanical calculating device. Writing to his friend Johannes Kepler, a famous astronomer, Schickard declared, "I have constructed a machine consisting of eleven complete and six partial sprocket wheels that can calculate." All copies of Schickard's device were lost or destroyed in the Thirty Years' War, however,

There are many different varieties of abacuses. On this one, each bead above the crossbar represents five units and each bead below represents one unit.

Wilhelm Schickard's reconstructed calculating machine

and Schickard and his family died in a plague epidemic. But Schickard had sent Kepler a sketch of his machine, which Kepler apparently used as a bookmark. It was discovered among Kepler's possessions more than 300 years later, and the device was reconstructed in 1960. It could add, subtract, multiply, and divide numbers of six or fewer digits.

The most famous early mechanical calculators were those built by the French philosopher Blaise Pascal (1623-1662). His father was a tax collector, and young Blaise wanted to make the job easier. In 1642, when he was just 19 years old, he invented an adding machine he called the Pascaline. Like the da Vinci and Schickard machines, the Pascaline used a series of interconnected wheels and gears. These were encased in a small wooden box with a set of eight dials on the front, each of which stood for a power of 10. Users would turn the dials with a stylus (a pen-shaped tool) to represent the numbers they wanted to add, and the answers would appear in small windows, where each digit was printed on a rotating cylinder that could be turned by the Pascaline's internal mechanics.

Pascal built about 50 Pascalines and attempted to sell them, but the business never took off. His devices were not very quick or reliable; they could add or (through a tedious process) subtract, but not multiply or divide. The Pascaline still became well known, however, and over the years it inspired other inventors. One of the most important of these was the German mathematician Gottfried Wilhelm

Like many early calculators, the shoebox-sized Pascaline was more often viewed as as an interesting conversation piece than a useful tool.

Leibniz (1646-1716), who constructed his own device in 1674. Leibniz's machine was capable of multiplication and division as well as addition and subtraction. It was also dependable and easy to build, because it was based on rotating drums rather than gears. Its existence was widely known, but somehow the device languished in a dusty university attic until 1879, when it was accidentally rediscovered by a work crew fixing the building's leaky roof.

The first commercially successful calculating device was developed in the nineteenth century by the Frenchman Charles Thomas de Colmar (1785-1870). His machine, called an arithmometer, used Leibniz-style drums rather than gears. This small

Leibniz said he created his machine "so that not only counting, but also addition and subtraction, multiplication and division could be accomplished by a suitably arranged machine easily, promptly, and with sure results."

wooden box—just 18 inches long, 7 inches wide and 3 inches deep—was only the first in a series that de Colmar produced. Although de Colmar's devices began to be sold around 1820, it wasn't until 1867 that they really became popular, after they were displayed at the Universal Exposition in Paris. Arithmometers remained in use until the 1910s.

De Colmar's most famous model was known as the "Piano Arithmometer," because it resembled a finely decorated piano in size and style.

All these mechanical calculating devices were a great improvement over the pen-and-paper method, but they shared one major problem: they required a lot of human participation to operate correctly. With the possible exception of the abacus, they were only good for performing a single calculation at a time. Someone had to set them up all over again for the next problem, and this created a possibility that the user could introduce an error. Since complex scientific and engineering problems required many individual calculations, the chances of making a mistake somewhere along the way were very high.

In the early nineteenth century, changes in manufacturing and industry increased the need for calculating machines. Industries once based on manual labor (such as weaving textiles) became mechanized, requiring more calculations. These advancements in manufacturing also meant that methods now existed to create better calculating machines. The time was ripe for a big jump forward in the field of automatic calculation. Over the next 150 years, many great thinkers tried their hands at designing better computing technology. This book profiles some of the most successful innovators in that field.

At first, these inventors' machines were thought to have very limited uses. Charles Babbage designed his Analytical Engine to improve mathematical tables, Alan Turing thought up his Turing machine to solve a mathematical puzzle, and John Mauchly and J. Presper Eckert built their ENIAC to aid the military during World War II. These early devices were not even called "computers." That word referred to the people who performed calculations by hand. It was only later, as new inventions freed human workers from such painstaking tasks, that the machines themselves were called computers. And eventually, their uses broadened beyond calculation. Jack Kilby and Robert Noyce, who invented the integrated circuit, and Ted Hoff, inventor of the microprocessor, helped computers become faster and more powerful than ever before—and just as importantly, they helped them become smaller and more affordable for businesses and individuals. After Steve Wozniak created Apple personal computers in the 1970s, everyday people began realizing how helpful computers could be for word processing, financial planning, and even game playing. Tim Berners-Lee expanded the uses of personal computers still further when he invented the World Wide Web, giving users access to new forms of research, entertainment, and communication.

The earliest of these innovators, Babbage and Turing, worked largely alone. Their machines were never built, and their achievements were not fully recognized until after their deaths. Later computer pioneers, such as Mauchly and Eckert, worked for universities and governments, the only institutions where funding was available to build their huge, complex creations—and where large amounts of data needed to be processed. As computers proved their usefulness, however, companies began forming to produce and sell them. Kilby, Noyce, and Hoff all worked for large electronics corporations that made millions of dollars marketing their inventions. Some inventors, including Noyce and Wozniak, even founded their own wildly successful companies. While computing grew as a science, it also became an important and lucrative industry that attracted thousands of new potential innovators.

Computers and their creators have changed over time, but their history remains important. We think of computers as marvels of modern technology, and they are. Certainly the feats we can perform with them today would have seemed magical to someone living a century or two ago. In reality, though, each new development was built upon those before it. The chain of responsibility for the computers we use every day, even the computers this book was written on, extends back in a clearly traceable line to those ancient farmers with their clay tokens. We'll never know anything about those early innovators; their identities will always remain a mystery to us, but they were just as important to today's computer-driven world as any of the inventors in this book. Consider this, then, not only a biography of the inventors we know about, but also an indirect tribute to those we don't.

CHAPTER ONE

Charles Babbage and the Analytical Engine

In the summer of 1821, two young men sat in the drawing room of a London gentleman's home. One was the gentleman himself, Charles Babbage. The other was John Herschel, an astronomer friend from college. The two pored over a stack of papers containing mathematical tables, carefully examining a set for possible errors.

In the days before mass-produced calculators, people who needed to perform complex calculations often referred to published tables of data in which the answers had already been figured out. The navy used navigational tables, insurance companies used statistics tables, bankers used interest-rate tables, and engineers used measurement-conversion tables. A single table could take up several volumes, and one tiny error could throw an entire calculation off by a large margin. Unfortunately, most published tables were riddled with mistakes. All of them were calculated by hand, usually by a pair of clerks (called

Although his inventions were never fully completed, Charles Babbage (1791-1871) dedicated much of his life to designing and building sophisticated calculating machines that were the forerunners of modern computers.

"An undetected error in a . . . table is like a sunken rock at sea yet undiscovered, upon which it is impossible to say what wrecks may have taken place," said John Herschel (1792-1871).

"computers") who worked independently of each other. The two sets of results were compared to check for mistakes, and then the lists were copied out and given to printers for typesetting. Errors could be made at any stage of this process.

Babbage and Herschel were revising the tables in the *Nautical Almanac* for the Astronomical Society, a group they had cofounded. That day, the friends compared supposedly identical tables calculated by two different clerks. Line by line, hour after hour, they called out numbers and marked errors. Finally, when he could take no more of the drudgery, Babbage exclaimed, "I wish to God these calculations had been executed by steam!" He would wrestle with this idea for the rest of his life. Charles Babbage never created a steam-powered calculating machine, but he did invent devices more advanced than any before them.

Charles Babbage was born in England on December 26, 1791, the first of four children of Benjamin and Elizabeth Babbage. (Two of the younger siblings died in infancy, leaving only Charles and his sister, Mary Anne.) Benjamin Babbage was a wealthy banker who could afford the best private education for young Charles. Much of Charles's youth was spent indulging his love of mathematics and other intellectual pursuits. By 1810, when he enrolled in Trinity College at Cambridge University, he was already an accomplished mathematician. Feeling that his professors were not as talented in the subject as he was, he founded the Analytical Society with some fellow students to study new mathematical theories and techniques.

After he graduated in spring 1814, Charles Babbage married his fiancée, Georgiana Whitmore, and moved to London to devote himself to a life of philosophy and science. His professional interests were extremely varied, even by the standards of the day. He eventually published 6 books and 86 papers on subjects as diverse as politics, life insurance, railroads, and code breaking. Babbage also developed useful inventions, including an automatic lighthouse signaling mechanism, a machine to play ticktacktoe, and the ophthalmoscope (a device for examining the retina that is still used today). In 1815, he became a member of the prestigious Royal Society of scientists.

Babbage had a reputation as a blunt, abrasive man. He lived for his work, and that made him hard

At 16, Charles Babbage attempted to invent shoes to walk on water. He nearly drowned when he tried them, however, and later remembered, "Ever after, when in the water, I preferred trusting to my own unassisted powers."

The Babbages had a daughter, Georgiana, and seven sons: Benjamin (who was always called by his middle name, Herschel), Charles Jr., Dugald, Henry, and three who died as infants. Tragically, Charles Jr. died in 1827 at the age of 10, and his mother followed a month later. Then, in 1834, Babbage's 17-year-old daughter passed away. Devastated by these losses, Babbage threw even more energy into his work.

Street musicians in London infuriated Babbage with their "racket," and for much of his life, he kept up a running feud with them. At first he bribed the musicians to play elsewhere, but then he began reporting them to the police. In return, they frequently staged loud, disharmonious performances near the Babbage house. The hostility continued for years, even while Babbage lay on his deathbed.

In Babbage's time, the word "engine" meant any sort of mechanical machine.

to get along with. He insisted, for example, that his wife care for their children herself, so he could concentrate solely on his work. He tolerated no outside disruptions.

Babbage may have been a cantankerous human being, but he was also a brilliant mathematician. After his exclamation in 1821 about doing calculations automatically, he became obsessed with the idea. By the spring of 1822, he had built a small working prototype of a device that he called the Difference Engine.

Babbage's intricate machine was designed to compute mathematical tables using the method of differences, a well-known technique that allowed people to solve complex functions by converting them into a series of addition problems. It would be too difficult, Babbage realized, to create a machine that could multiply and divide large numbers, but addition was a process simple enough to be performed mechanically. Besides its simplicity, the method of differences offered another advantage: it used each result to perform the next addition problem in the series. Instead of proofreading an entire table, the user of the Difference Engine simply had to check the final number the machine produced. As long as it was correct, all the other numbers were guaranteed to be correct as well.

In Babbage's plan for the Difference Engine, a series of wheels mounted on vertical rods were each inscribed with the numbers zero to nine. Each wheel represented one digit of a number (ones, tens, hundreds, etc.), and the rotation of the wheel determined the digit's value. Babbage planned to have enough wheels to handle numbers of about 20 digits. The machine's operator would turn the wheels by hand to set the starting values. Then the operator pulled a handle to set the parts in motion. With every pull, the wheels moved automatically to perform repeated addition. Each cycle of the engine produced a result based on the one before it. Babbage's design even included a sort of printer—a system to impress the results into thin strips of metal or other soft materials, which could then be used on a printing press. This feature eliminated the possibility that errors might be made in copying down the results or setting them in type.

Babbage introduced his Difference Engine at an Astronomical Society meeting in June 1822. He also described the device to the head of the Royal Society in a letter that was printed and distributed throughout London. The British government heard of the invention and asked the Royal Society to judge its worth. The Society's members replied in May 1823 that Babbage was "highly deserving of public encouragement in . . . his arduous undertaking." Hoping the Difference Engine could improve navigational tables for the Royal Navy, the government agreed to fund the construction of a full-scale machine. Two months later, the Astronomical Society awarded Babbage its first gold medal in recognition of his invention.

Babbage spent the next decade struggling to turn his prototype into the perfect calculating machine. He received some government grants, but

After reading about Babbage's Difference Engine in a magazine, Swedish printer Georg Scheutz and his son Edvard built a similar device in 1843. Because the article did not describe the machine in detail, they used Babbage's concepts, but an entirely different design. Babbage enthusiastically endorsed the Scheutz engine, and it won a gold medal at the Paris Exposition in 1855. Unfortunately, the machine did not prove its worth financially or technically, and both Georg and Edvard eventually died bankrupt. Their Difference Engine is now owned by the Smithsonian Institution.

At the time Babbage broke with Clement, about 12,000 Difference Engine parts had been completed. The calculating section of the machine was mostly complete, but the printer was not.

ended up using mostly his own money. His design for the Difference Engine called for about 25,000 parts, many of which needed to be nearly identical. At the time, mass-production technology was not yet established, so each part had to be created by hand. The craftsmen that Babbage hired often had to develop new tools and techniques before they could even begin to make the parts.

Babbage was challenged not only by the difficulty of his task, but also by his own perfectionism. Often, just as he completed a portion of the engine's design, he would think of a more efficient way to do the same thing and start all over again. Months became years. Government officials, concerned about the money they had provided, pressured Babbage to move faster. Then, in 1832, a billing dispute flared between Babbage and his star engineer, Joseph Clement. Clement held the machine parts and detailed technical drawings in his possession, and he refused to work or to return them until Babbage paid his bill. The conflict wore on for 16 months, and eventually Babbage and Clement parted ways.

During this period of enforced idleness, Babbage began to ponder his Difference Engine's flaws. It was the most advanced calculating device of its time, and it would have done its job of calculating tables beautifully. But it could perform only addition. Its arrangement of rods and gears was useless for any other kind of work. Babbage realized that as wonderful as the Difference Engine was, he could do much, much better.

THE BREAKTHROUGH

Every previous calculating machine had been designed to perform a specific type of calculation. But between the summers of 1834 and 1836, Babbage designed a machine that would be able to solve virtually any type of mathematical problem, provided the operator gave it instructions on how to do it. The Analytical Engine, as he called it, would be an all-purpose computing machine.

The Analytical Engine was unique in its shape as well as its purpose. Babbage changed the Difference Engine's crib-like arrangement of rods to a circular pattern, which allowed the results of a computation to be automatically fed back into the machine and used for the next round of processing. This design—which Babbage compared to "a loco-motive that lays down its own railway"—required less intervention from the operator and added multiplication and division to the machine's abilities. The most crucial innovation Babbage developed, however, was splitting the machine into different components—a remarkably similar design to modern computers. The engine's "mill" (or processor) was responsible for carrying out the calculations, while the "store" (or memory) stored the numbers upon which the mill would operate. Babbage envisioned a store capable of holding 1,000 numbers of 50 digits each. To perform a calculation, the mill looked up a number on a rack from the store, used it to work the problem, and stashed the result back in the store.

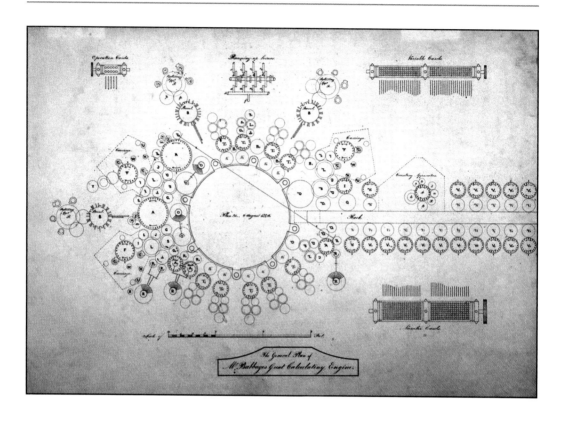

This plan for the Analytical Engine shows its circular arrangement, which Babbage described as "the Engine eating its own tail."

Separating the machine's functions into different areas made it much more efficient.

Babbage realized that the process of putting data in and getting results out had to be improved. He planned a number of extra components to be added as needed, including an improved version of the Difference Engine's printer and a device for drawing curves based on mathematical functions. He also designed a component to record data for later use onto punch cards, as well as another that could read the cards back in. This card reader was an especially important innovation. The cards were bits of pasteboard, all the same size, with patterns of holes punched in them. When a card was placed in the engine, a matrix of rods would push against it. Where there was a hole in the card, a rod would pass through; where there was no hole, the rod would be blocked. With the rods sensing the unique pattern of holes in each card, the engine could "read" the card's value. A series of cards could be strung together with small wire loops so that once the operator fed in the first card, the engine could pull in the rest of the cards by itself. Today, this string of cards would be called a program.

> **program:** a detailed set of instructions that tells a computer which operations to perform and in what order

The Analytical Engine used four types of cards. Operation cards instructed the mill to perform a certain type of calculation encoded on the card. Variable cards told the mill which value to fetch from the store or where to place the results of a computation. Number cards held numerical constants. Since the engine's store could hold relatively few numbers at one time, large calculations might temporarily require more storage space. The machine could punch a value onto a number card, then read it again later when it was needed. This technique effectively increased the size of the store. The fourth type of card was called a combinatorial card. Because all the cards in a program were strung together, the engine's card reader could either advance to the next card or return to a previous one. Combinatorial cards determined which way to move the cards and how far, allowing the engine to run certain parts of its program repeatedly. Today, this method is known as "looping." It made Babbage's creation the first programmable mechanical computer.

This portion of the mill was one of the few completed parts of the Analytical Engine. "The Engine is unfortunately far too much in advance of my own country to meet with the least support," complained Babbage in 1841. "I have at an expense of many thousands of pounds caused the drawings to be executed, and I have carried on experiments for its perfection. Unless however some country more enlightened than my own should take up the subject, there is no chance of that machine ever being executed during my own life."

THE RESULT

The Analytical Engine could have been one of the crowning achievements of the nineteenth century. But the British government wanted its Difference Engine, and Babbage never completed one. The government was therefore unwilling to provide further funding for his new project, and the job was too costly to undertake himself. In fact, for many years historians believed Babbage's Analytical Engine would have been impossible to build at the time. Its parts had to be manufactured so precisely that they seemed beyond nineteenth-century technology. At a time when every tiny nut, bolt, screw, and gear was individually handcrafted, artisans could not create

the immense number of identical parts required to build an Analytical Engine. And that, the argument went, is why Babbage's innovation remained confined to paper.

Nonetheless, the Analytical Engine did achieve some fame in its time. In 1840, having worked out much of the design, Babbage went to a scientific conference in Turin, Italy, that was attended by many members of Europe's scientific and engineering elite. Babbage gave a series of lectures in his lodgings on his Analytical Engine. He talked for hours, eager to explain his work to those who he knew could appreciate it—and appreciate it they did. During his stay in Italy, Babbage received numerous honorary titles and memberships in scientific societies. Best of all, Luigi Menabrea, an Italian mathematician who attended Babbage's lectures in Turin and took copious notes, published the first public account of the Analytical Engine in 1842. The article was written in French, however, so it was not widely read in England.

In early 1843, Babbage's friend Augusta Ada, countess of Lovelace, presented him with her English translation of Menabrea's article. Lovelace was herself an accomplished mathematician, and at Babbage's suggestion, she added her own commentary to the article and published it in August 1843. Her translation and her extra notes—which were more than twice as long as the original article—helped publicize Babbage's invention in his own country.

For the rest of his life, Babbage continually tinkered with his plans for the Analytical Engine, but he never built more than a few small parts. In

Augusta Ada Byron Lovelace (1815-1852) was the only legitimate child of the famous poet Lord Byron, but her parents separated when she was only a month old, and she never knew her father. When she met Charles Babbage, she was 17—around the same age as his own daughter, Georgiana (who died shortly thereafter)—and she developed a strong father-daughter relationship with him.

1842, he produced a completely new set of drawings for a "Difference Engine #2," building on the techniques he discovered while designing the Analytical Engine. Although the new design still relied on the method of differences, the mechanics were more efficient, performing the same computations with one-third the number of parts.

On October 18, 1871, two months before his 80th birthday, Charles Babbage died in his home. There were few mourners at his funeral. Later, his son Henry—who had come to have a good working knowledge of both the Difference Engine and Analytical Engine plans—managed to build five or six small demonstration pieces out of spare parts, including part of the Analytical Engine's mill. But by his own death, Henry had assembled only six pieces. He donated them to various universities around the world. The rest of the spare parts were auctioned off or melted down for scrap metal.

For many years, Charles Babbage's work was forgotten. His manuscripts and notebooks lay unstudied until the 1970s, more than 30 years after the invention of the modern computer. Because it was lost for so long, Babbage's work did not influence the development of computers as we know them today. A few pioneers of early electronic computers claim to have been aware of Babbage's work, but most deny that Babbage's ideas shaped their own. That has not stopped him, however, from becoming one of the central figures in the history of computing. He is recognized as the first to have invented— in the sense of "conceived of"—a computer. Now

Howard Aiken, designer of the Harvard Mark I, the first electromechanical computer, claimed to have been inspired by one of Henry Babbage's engine pieces. Harvard was the final resting place of one of these pieces, but some historians doubt Aiken's claim.

Babbage's name is better known, more respected, and even more revered than ever, especially among computer scientists.

In 1985, the Science Museum of London decided to try to disprove the theory that Babbage's designs were beyond the technology of his day. Using the drawings for the Difference Engine #2, and employing only manufacturing methods and materials that would have been available in Babbage's time, the museum began constructing the first full Babbage machine ever to be built. The project took nearly seven years to complete. On November 29, 1991, after weeks of debugging and less than a month before Babbage's 200th birthday, his engine performed its first successful calculation, determining the first 100 powers of 7. It performed flawlessly.

Engineers Barrie Holloway (left) and Reg Crick, who built the calculating part of Babbage's Difference Engine #2, prepare it for display in the Science Museum of London in 1991.

CHAPTER TWO

Alan Turing
and the Turing Machine

Computers, though they are all basically the same, are capable of a virtually unlimited number of tasks. We can thank Alan Turing for this flexibility— Alan Turing, and a machine that never existed.

Alan Mathison Turing was born in London on June 23, 1912. His parents, Julius and Ethel Turing, lived mostly in India, where Julius was part of the British colonial government. Alan's parents believed the Indian heat would be bad for their sons' health, so Alan and his older brother, John, were left in the care of family friends. Their parents returned to England only for the occasional family vacation.

Alan was an exceptionally intelligent boy, teaching himself to read in only three weeks. He excelled at French and used it as a secret code to keep others from reading the postcards he sent to his mother. But Alan loved mathematics and science best of all. When he was very young, he stopped at every lamppost and read the numbers on it, just to

An imaginary machine inspired Alan Turing (1912-1954) to make very real advances in computer science.

prove he could. When he was 12, he got a chemistry set for Christmas. He spent hours at the beach near the family home, gathering pounds of seaweed. From it, he extracted a tiny amount of iodine to use in his experiments.

In May 1926, when Alan was 13, his parents enrolled him at a boarding school called Sherborne. (Americans would refer to Sherborne as a private school, because it admitted only those students it wanted to attend and charged tuition and fees. In England, however, such schools are called public schools.) Alan's grades there were poor; he even had trouble in his favorite subjects because he preferred his own ways of solving problems to those taught by his teachers. Part of the reason may have been that the school focused on Greek, Latin, and literature, not science and math. The headmaster wrote of young Alan's poor grades, "If he is to stay at a Public School, he must aim at becoming educated. If he is to be solely a Scientific Specialist, he is wasting his time at a Public School."

At first, Alan had few friends at Sherborne. He was aloof and awkward in social situations and team sports. In 1927, however, he met Christopher Morcom. Christopher, a year older, shared Alan's love of science and math. But while Alan was shy and self-conscious, Christopher was confident and made friends easily. While Alan had trouble adapting to life at Sherborne, Christopher thrived. Their friendship seemed unlikely, but it flourished. The boys challenged each other to solve difficult math problems and eagerly discussed their scientific

Although he didn't like team sports, Turing was not physically inept. He enjoyed walking, running, and cycling, and he pursued these activities his whole life. As an adult, he preferred to bike to work rather than ride in a car, and he would sometimes schedule his lectures and speaking engagements in such a way that he could give the first lecture and then run several miles to give the second.

discoveries. Alan later wrote of his friend, "He made everyone else seem so ordinary." When Christopher died suddenly from tuberculosis in February 1930, Alan was devastated. He believed that if Christopher's life had not been cut short, his intelligence and effortless popularity would have led him to do great things. Since Christopher couldn't do them, Alan felt it was up to him. He applied himself to his studies as never before. In the autumn of 1930, he was even appointed prefect of his house, a position of influence and leadership.

Alan Turing graduated from Sherborne in 1931 and won a scholarship to prestigious King's College at Cambridge University, where he found a new world of opportunities in math and science. Surrounded by many of the brilliant mathematicians of his time, Turing pursued the most challenging courses the university could offer. By the spring of 1935, when he was only 22, he was so well regarded that he was elected a fellow of King's College. Fellowships were a way for the college to promote innovative new work from the most promising researchers. Fellows, also known as dons, were given free room and board and a modest salary, and they were allowed to pursue their own research for up to six years. It was a tremendous honor, particularly for someone as young as Turing.

While finishing his studies at Cambridge, Turing attended a lecture that was to have a profound impact on his work. The lecturer discussed the work of David Hilbert, one of the most influential mathematicians of the time. Born in 1862,

To honor Turing's achievement, the boys back at Sherborne were given a half-day holiday. One of them penned a short tribute:
"Turing
Must have been alluring
To get made a don
So early on."

proof: a strict, step-by-step demonstration that clearly shows the truth of a mathematical statement

Hilbert made discoveries in several mathematical fields, including Euclidean geometry and algebraic number theory. In 1928, he had posed a very challenging question: given a mathematical statement, is there a way to know whether it is provable, without first having to prove it?

Mathematicians use proofs to show whether a statement is true. For example, $2 + 2 = 4$ is easily provable, because the definition of adding numbers together means two plus two does equal four. On the other hand, $2 + 2 = 5$ is not provable, since there is no way to add the two numbers and get a result of five—that's not how addition works. These are very simple examples, and proving them takes so little effort that it would be a waste of time to try to find out in advance if they're provable. But mathematicians deal with much more difficult statements, ones that can take months, years, or even decades to prove. If it were possible to decide in advance whether a statement could be proved, without having to go through the trouble of proving it, it would be an enormous discovery. Unfortunately, no one knew if this was possible.

THE BREAKTHROUGH

Hilbert's question stuck in Turing's mind. One summer day in 1935, lying in a meadow and gazing up at the sky while resting during an afternoon run, Turing realized a way to answer it.

Turing imagined a machine much like a typewriter. His imaginary machine would read symbols written on a paper tape of infinite length that was divided into small squares of equal size. Each square would either contain a symbol or be blank. Depending on the symbol, Turing's machine could take some action. It could move the tape forward to the next square, move it backwards to the previous square, write a new symbol, or erase the symbol entirely. This imagined tape worked much like what we now call a program, describing a complete set of operations. If the same tape were fed into the machine several times, it would always take the same steps and arrive at the same outcome. Turing knew that the key to this repeatability was the fact that the machine was deterministic—its output was decided entirely by the markings on the tape. There was no way it could deviate from the plan and do something unique, or arrive at a different result. Given the right tape, Turing's machine could, theoretically, compute anything that was computable.

Turing also imagined a list of all possible valid programs for his machine. He devised a way to translate even the most complex set of instructions into a single very large number. Turing imagined that the number worked as a program that any properly set-up machine could run. But there is an infinite amount of large numbers, and not every one of them can be a valid program. Some numbers would not be "understood" by the machine to be instructions. Turing wondered how he could tell the difference between a number that was a valid program and a number that wasn't. If he picked a random number, he realized, he'd certainly get a program, but a program to do what? Would it do anything useful? Would it compute something, or would it just repeat itself endlessly, moving the imaginary tape back and forth without ever producing an answer? Turing realized there was no way to know in advance whether a given number would produce a valid program. He might be able to produce a test that would work on some numbers, but he could never produce one that would work on all numbers. The only way to know for sure if a given number was a valid program would be to run the number as a program and see what happened.

Remember Hilbert's original question: can it be known whether a mathematical statement is provable, without having to prove it? Turing asked exactly the same question, but using slightly different words: can it be known whether a given program will ever finish, without having to run it? By answering his own question with a resounding "no," Turing also answered Hilbert's question, one that had stumped the world's best minds for years. Hilbert had believed that all mathematical problems could be solved. Turing's imaginary machine, however, demonstrated that there was such a thing as an unsolvable problem—a program that never finished.

The question of whether a given program will ever finish is now called the "halting problem" by computer scientists.

THE RESULT

Turing's machine was designed solely to answer Hilbert's question. In order to do that, though, he had to prove that it could compute anything that was computable, as long as it was provided with the proper instruction tape. It was a machine capable of undertaking an almost infinite number of different jobs, if told exactly how to do so. Sound a lot like a modern computer? That is no coincidence. The imaginary "Turing machine" would provide the foundation upon which Turing and others would eventually build the first electronic digital computers.

In January 1937, when Turing was just 25, he published his answer to Hilbert's question in a landmark paper called "On Computable Numbers," which appeared in the *Proceedings of the London Mathematical Society*. While preparing his paper for publication, Turing learned of a professor in the United States at Princeton University, Alonzo Church, who shared his interests. In fact, Church had also arrived at the same answer to Hilbert's question at about the same time, but in a different way. Turing traveled to the United States and enrolled at Princeton as a Ph.D. student to study with Church.

At Princeton, Turing began applying his mathematical talent to ciphers—codes that can prevent a message from being read by anyone other than its creator and its intended recipient. He had been fascinated by ciphers since childhood, but it had been a hobby. Now ciphers became his serious work. He believed that coding and decoding messages might be a good example of a task that could be performed by a Turing machine. After graduating in 1938, Turing returned to England, where he probably discussed his cipher work with other scholars at King's College, some of whom were on the staff of the Government Code & Cipher School (GC&CS). GC&CS hired Turing to work part-time on special projects, and it is this work that Turing is perhaps most famous for today. Started during World War I as "Room 40," GC&CS helped the British government create its own codes and decipher the codes of other nations. The radio messages airplanes and ships used to communicate could be heard by anyone with a radio receiver, so they had to be disguised if they contained strategic information. Encoding and decoding the messages was laborious work, but there was no other option—especially during wartime.

In the 1930s, nations watched Germany's military buildup with concern. Britain intercepted German radio messages to keep track of what was happening. But in 1937, the Germans started using a new code to encrypt all their military radio messages. It was created by a device known as the Enigma machine, a small box like a typewriter with a row of lights at the top, a series of removable wheels called rotors, and a set of changeable circuits called a plugboard. Three times a day, German radio operators scrambled the plugboard connections and placed the rotors in a different starting position. The plugboard settings and rotor positions were secret, known only to radiomen in the field and those they communicated with at headquarters. To encode a message, an operator typed it on the keyboard. For each key pressed, electricity flowed from the key, through the rotors and plugboard, to a light at the top. Each light corresponded with a letter. Typing an "h," for example, might cause the letter "u" to light up; "u" would then be transmitted. At the other end, the coded message was typed into a receiving Enigma machine with the same settings, which would decode it.

Each rotor contained different electrical pathways, so rotors in different positions caused different letters to light up. Not only could the three rotors be removed and replaced in any order, but they also turned with each press of a key. Even if the same key were struck several times in a row, it would produce a different coded letter every time—almost like using

Three rotors in the Enigma machine could produce 105,456 different alphabetical substitutions. For each of these, there were 1.3 trillion different ways of connecting just seven pairs of letters on the plugboard. The possible codes were almost limitless. The pictured machine holds four rotors.

Deciphering German naval communications was especially important because German submarines were sinking the Allied ships that brought food and other necessary supplies to embattled Britain. Once the Enigma code was broken, the Allies could pinpoint the position of the submarines and avoid them. Suddenly unable to sink many enemy ships, the Germans became suspicious. They still believed, however, that the Enigma code was unbreakable, so they assumed that a spy was leaking the ship positions.

In 1946, Turing was honored with the Order of the British Empire, an award for distinguished service to the crown. But he was never allowed to tell his friends or family exactly what he had done during the war to earn the honor.

a separate code for each letter. Later, the Germans added two more rotors. Although only three could be used at a time, there were five to choose from, making the code even more complex. With so many possible combinations of rotor and plugboard positions, the Enigma code seemed unbreakable.

When World War II began in 1939, deciphering the German radio messages became a matter of the highest importance to Britain. The GC&CS staff quadrupled and was secretly housed in an old mansion called Bletchley Park located northwest of London. Turing was one of those who came aboard full time. His job was to design a machine capable of breaking the Enigma code. A team of Polish mathematicians had made a machine that could crack the codes of a less powerful, prewar version of Enigma, one that lacked a plugboard. The Polish machine automatically checked a large number of possible rotor settings, and it would stop when it found the right one. Because it was constantly ticking, its designers called it a "bombe."

Based on this design, Turing and his colleague Gordon Welchman were able to produce an improved bombe—one that was up to the challenge posed by the more complex version of Enigma. By 1942, thanks in large part to this machine and others inspired by Turing, GC&CS deciphered up to 84,000 German messages a month, almost two every minute. The codebreakers saved many lives and considerably shortened the war in Europe. But because of military secrecy, most of them, including Turing, were never publicly recognized for their heroic work.

After the war, Turing continued to work on and off at GC&CS. He was also employed by the National Physical Laboratory (NPL) to design and build an electronic digital computer. Turing submitted a design for a device he called the Automatic Computing Engine (ACE), which was much like his imaginary Turing machine. Instead of an infinite paper tape, though, the ACE would have a finite amount of memory. Because the memory would store both the program and the data, the ACE was known as a stored-program computer. Stringing together a small set of simple instructions, it would have been capable of running very complex programs. Turing's colleagues, however, thought the

Enigma was the most famous German code, but another inspired the creation of one of the earliest programmable electronic computers. In 1943, Bletchley Park staff built a room-sized machine called Colossus, which scanned coded messages printed on paper tape and searched for patterns in the letters. Turing did not work directly on the project, but it was inspired by his Turing machine idea and demonstrated to him the potential of electronics.

Turing (right) and colleagues at the console of a Ferranti Mark I computer

design too ambitious and hard to build. Instead, NPL agreed to build a much smaller version, the Pilot Model ACE. Then its construction encountered a series of delays.

On June 21, 1948, the world's first stored-program electronic digital computer executed its first program. Unfortunately for Turing, it was not his Pilot Model ACE, but the Manchester Mark I Prototype, built at the University of Manchester by a competing team. Frustrated by the delays at NPL, Turing left for Manchester, where he became deputy director of the Royal Society Computing Machine Laboratory. There, he helped to turn the small Mark I Prototype into a full-sized machine. By February 1951, the Ferranti company was manufacturing copies of the Mark I, making it the first commercially

available electronic digital computer. That same year, Turing was honored as a Fellow of the Royal Society of London, which recognized that Turing machines had become the basis of electronic computing.

Despite his professional achievements, Turing never felt that he fit in well with society, and each success was met with deepening personal depression. On June 7, 1954, at his home in Manchester, Alan Turing committed suicide by eating an apple he had dipped in a home-brewed cyanide solution. But despite Turing's tragic end, his work had a profound impact on the fields of mathematics and what would become computer science. His papers are still required reading at many universities, and his Turing machines were the blueprint for modern computers.

CHAPTER THREE

John Mauchly and J. Presper Eckert and the Electronic Computer

When John Mauchly was a child in the 1910s, he loved to read in bed at night, long after he was supposed to have been asleep. His bedroom was on the second floor, and as his parents came upstairs, they could see under his door and tell whether his light was on. So young John solved his problem ingeniously: he wired the landing at the bottom of the stairs to a small light bulb in his room. When his parents started up the stairs, the small light would go out, giving him time to turn off the main light. When his parents went back downstairs, the bulb came back on, indicating that it was safe to read again.

John Mauchly couldn't have known it yet, but there was at least one other boy with the same passion for electronics. John Presper Eckert, known as "Pres," was interested in the subject even as a small child. Pres liked to draw circuit diagrams on whatever scraps of paper he could get his hands on,

During their nearly decade-long inventing partnership, John Mauchly (1907-1980; right) and J. Presper Eckert (1919-1995) built the earliest electronic computers.

At the age of five, John Mauchly built a flashlight from a battery and a light bulb and used it to explore his friend's dark attic. When he was older, he took advantage of new construction in his neighborhood to put intercom wires in the trenches workmen used to lay pipes. He and his friends could use the wires to communicate from house to house.

including the backs of restaurant checks. It would be years before Pres Eckert and John Mauchly finally met, but when they did, they would team up to create the world's first fully electronic computer.

John William Mauchly was born in Cincinnati, Ohio, on August 30, 1907, to Sebastian and Rachel Mauchly. Sebastian worked as a high-school principal, but he was a physicist by training. In 1916, the family moved to Chevy Chase, Maryland, when Sebastian took a position with the prestigious Carnegie Institution in Washington, D.C. As the new chief physicist for the Institution's Department of Terrestrial Magnetism, he studied physics as it related to Earth and its weather, a fascination he passed on to his son.

While he was still a youth, John Mauchly became an expert in electricity and electronics. Whenever anyone in the neighborhood had a wiring problem, they called him to fix it—and since home electrical wiring was still relatively new at the time, problems were frequent. In the autumn of 1925, Mauchly enrolled at Johns Hopkins University to study engineering, but he soon grew bored. He complained that it was simply rote work with little chance to be creative. "Physicists," he said, "those were the boys who were going to have fun." Fortunately for Mauchly, Johns Hopkins had a special program that allowed gifted students to start their advanced graduate degrees without completing their bachelor's degrees first. Just two years after entering the engineering program, Mauchly began studying graduate physics, and in 1932 he earned his Ph.D. After a year working as a research assistant at Johns Hopkins, he took a job as the only professor in the physics department at Ursinus College, near Philadelphia.

While Mauchly was at Ursinus, his hobby was studying the physics of weather. Mauchly had easy access to a large amount of data generated by the U.S. Weather Bureau, but analyzing it required many statistical calculations, too many for a human to perform in any reasonable amount of time. Mauchly became interested in designing and building an electrical calculating machine that could process the information. In 1941, he heard that the University of Pennsylvania's Moore School of Electrical Engineering was offering a 10-week crash course for those holding degrees in related fields. He enrolled, and although he was the oldest student, he was assigned to do his laboratory work with the youngest instructor—J. Presper Eckert.

"Pres," born on April 9, 1919, was the son of John Eckert, a wealthy real-estate developer. John Sr. was part of Philadelphia's social and economic elite. He traveled extensively and often brought young Pres with him to meet famous people of the day. Pres, however, was more interested in science than in superstars. When he was 12 years old, he won first prize in a local science fair by building a remote-controlled boat that floated in a large basin of water. He used strong electromagnets under the basin to steer the boat, and he was even able to devise a mechanism by which a magnet could "drop" one boat, then "pick up" another and control it

The course that Mauchly took was called "Defense Training in Electronics," and it was sponsored by the U.S. War Department. The country was preparing to enter World War II, and it needed trained technicians to work on radar, radios, and other military machines.

As a youngster, during a golf trip with his father, Pres was photographed with President Warren G. Harding. John and Pres were even known to hang out on movie sets with two big stars of the time, Douglas Fairbanks and Charlie Chaplin.

instead. During high school, he spent time in the labs of Philo T. Farnsworth, who in 1927 had invented the modern television system.

In addition to his skill with electronics, Pres Eckert was a whiz in mathematics. When he took the College Board examinations, a standard part of applying for admission to a college, he earned the nation's second-highest score in the math section, ranking just behind one of his own classmates. He wanted to attend the Massachusetts Institute of Technology, the most prestigious engineering and technical school in the U.S. But his parents preferred that he study business, so he enrolled in the University of Pennsylvania's Wharton School of Business. He quickly became bored, though, and transferred to the University's Moore School of Electrical Engineering, where he earned his bachelor's degree in 1941.

When Eckert graduated, he stayed on as an instructor. He was John Mauchly's electronics teacher, even though he was 12 years younger than his student. Mauchly was soon hired as a professor at the Moore School, and the two became colleagues. They formed a fast friendship, the focus of which was electronics and designing machines to do computation. They would often talk and sketch for hours at a time, figuring out ways to make the existing calculating devices faster and more efficient.

Most of the advanced calculating machines of the day were mechanical: they relied on the motion of gears or switches to do their work. The one used at the Moore School, the Differential Analyzer, was a giant, complex system of wheels and shafts driven by electric motors. It was designed to handle only one type of mathematical problem, and setting it up for a computation could take up to two days, sometimes longer than it would have taken to work out the answer by hand. Electromechanical devices, used in research labs across the country, were somewhat faster. Instead of gears, some of them relied on fast electronic switches called relays, originally designed for use by telephone companies. But even a fast relay required a certain amount of time to switch positions, and that slowed the machine down considerably. Eckert and Mauchly knew that the best way to improve speed was to eliminate the moving parts altogether.

The first Differential Analyzer was developed at MIT by Vannevar Bush in the 1930s.

THE BREAKTHROUGH

In August 1942, Mauchly wrote a seven-page report summarizing the pair's idea to use electronic devices called vacuum tubes to build a computing device. Originally invented by John Ambrose Fleming in 1904, vacuum tubes were in wide use in the electronics industry by the 1940s. They were particularly useful in amplifying weak electrical signals, which made them perfect for radio and TV receivers. They could also be used as very fast switches. Mauchly and Eckert wanted to build a digital device in which numbers were represented by electrical pulses; the vacuum tubes would control and count the pulses to perform calculations. Unfortunately, vacuum tubes were notoriously unreliable, and many scientists saw the whole idea of fully electronic calculation as a crackpot scheme. When Mauchly submitted his report to his superiors at the Moore School, it was conveniently "lost."

A vacuum tube is a sealed glass or metal tube with most of the air removed. It has three electronic components: a cathode (or filament), an anode (or plate), and a grid to channel the flow of electricity between the two.

At this time, the Moore School was involved in a large project for the U.S. Army's Ballistics Research Laboratory in Aberdeen, Maryland. The U.S. was fighting World War II and had a desperate need for high-speed calculating machines. The armed forces relied on artillery guns that lobbed heavy explosive shells in long arcs through the air to their targets. The gunner had to judge the distance to the target, the weight of the shell, the weather conditions, and many other factors. No human could compute a shell's proper trajectory (path) quickly enough, especially during the heat of battle. Instead, the army supplied its gunners with precomputed tables that accounted for each of these variables.

Unfortunately, each piece of artillery equipment, type of shell, or even area of the world required the production of an entirely new set of tables. Calculating a single trajectory required about 750 individual multiplications, and each table had an average of 3,000 different trajectories. It took roughly 12 hours for a person to figure out a single trajectory, and about 1,500 days—more than four years—to compute an entire table. The Moore School used the Differential Analyzer to reduce that time to about a month. This was still much too slow for the army, which needed to get new tables to the troops as soon as possible. Faster tables were literally a life-or-death necessity, and Mauchly's designs promised to make them up to 1,000 times faster.

In early 1943, First Lieutenant Herman Goldstine, a mathematician, was assigned to oversee the Moore School's trajectory project. When a chance conversation with a graduate student brought Mauchly's idea for an electronic calculation to his attention, Goldstine was interested. Although the original report had been "lost," Mauchly quickly reconstructed it. By April, the army had approved the creation of a new project to produce an entirely electronic digital calculating machine, the Electronic Numerical Integrator and Computer (ENIAC). Eckert was made chief engineer of the project, Mauchly contributed much of the design, and engineers from the Moore School joined the team to build the world's first electronic computer.

In 1941, Mauchly had visited the lab of John V. Atanasoff, a professor of mathematics and physics at Iowa State University. Atanasoff and his student Clifford Berry had designed and built a small computing device for solving algebraic equations. The Atanasoff-Berry Computer (ABC) used about 300 vacuum tubes as switches. Although it never became fully operational and Mauchly thought he could do much better, the ABC confirmed that an electronic computer was a real and workable idea.

Mauchly was a physicist. He was interested in building whatever . . . would work in the shortest period of time. An engineer builds something so it can be manufactured and so it lasts. A physicist may use something only once, so he builds it out of any crap he can get his hands on. It could have been built out of ladies' hairpins. He just wanted something built. But Eckert had very rigorous standards. They complemented each other very well.
—Herman Goldstine

Eckert was so painstaking that he even studied mice to see which kinds of wire they enjoyed eating, then used the least appetizing wires in the ENIAC.

The engineers who designed and built the ENIAC gave little thought to how it would be programmed. Programming was considered boring drudgery, requiring technical skill but not much creativity. So the unglamorous job of being the world's first computer programmers fell to six female mathematicians: Frances Spence, Jean Bartik, Ruth Teitelbaum, Elizabeth Holberton, Marlyn Meltzer, and Kathleen McNulty.

Under immense pressure from the military to finish the project in time to help with the war effort, the ENIAC team worked seven days a week, nearly around the clock. When they became frustrated, they often referred to the machine as "MANIAC." At the time, it was probably the most complex device anyone had ever built. Not only did it have about 18,000 vacuum tubes, but it also had nearly 85,000 other electronic parts. If any single part failed, the computer wouldn't be able to do its job—and with more than 100,000 parts, each working rapidly, there were almost 500 million chances for the machine to fail every second. The ENIAC was huge, too. Fully assembled, it covered 1,800 square feet, about the size of a spacious three-bedroom apartment, and it weighed 30 tons.

The ENIAC was made up of around 40 individual pieces that looked like large metal cabinets full of switches and blinking lights. Each cabinet could perform a specific function. Some added, some multiplied, some did division. One unit connected the ENIAC to a punch-card reader for data input, and another connected to a card puncher for data output. There were also several portable function tables—large circuit panels on wheels. Programmers would use these to store numbers that went into the calculation. By flipping switches on a function table and connecting it to one of the other modules, they could specify variables (such as air density or shell weight) that would affect the artillery tables the ENIAC was designed to compute. The master programmer module controlled all these components.

If all this sounds complicated, that's because it was. Programming the ENIAC meant disconnecting all the modules from one another, then reconnecting them in a different sequence according to what sort of program was needed. Next, the programmers had to go to each module and flip a confusing array of switches to tell it what its role in the overall calculation would be and which numbers were initially stored there. To make matters even more difficult, the ENIAC could run for only five or six hours before it suffered a hardware failure, usually a burned-out vacuum tube. Fortunately, replacing one

The ENIAC's female programmers were not trained; they used the plans and asked the engineers questions to teach themselves how the complex system worked. "It was the most exciting work I ever did," said Jean Bartik, shown here (left) with Frances Bilas. "I loved working with the engineers. I loved going to work. The more you use your head, the more you enjoy your work."

hardware: the physical parts of a computer system, such as ENIAC's vacuum tubes or the CPU, disk drive, memory, keyboard, and monitor of a modern computer

In the end, building the ENIAC took 200,000 man-hours of work and cost $486,804.22.

vacuum tube didn't take very long, but it did mean the machine needed constant attention while it was running.

In a way, the ENIAC was simply a series of calculators wired together. But what made it greater than that was its ability to react to the data it produced. The master programmer could instruct the machine to perform an operation until something happened—for instance, until the results became negative numbers instead of positive ones. If the numbers remained positive, the ENIAC would keep running the operation. If the numbers became negative, then the machine would automatically move on to a new stage of its task. This "if . . . then" logic is a central feature of modern computers.

The ENIAC was finally finished sometime during the fall of 1945, just after the war ended. The army still needed trajectory tables, but the need wasn't as great in peacetime. Nevertheless, the ENIAC was an impressive achievement. The press was invited to a gala dedication ceremony on February 14, 1946. There were many speeches, a five-course dinner, and congratulations all around. The ENIAC demonstrated its jaw-dropping speed by computing an entire trajectory, 12 hours of work for a human, in only 30 seconds. It was 1,000 times faster than any calculator and 500 times faster than any existing computing machine. Shortly thereafter, the Moore School received an order for an identical machine from the Russian government, but it was turned down. The ENIAC was clearly too valuable for the U.S. to share.

THE RESULT

Despite the ENIAC's success, Eckert and Mauchly were not content. Their computer had been designed and built in a hurry, and it was clearly too complex. Different circuits had been created by different groups of engineers working independently of one another. The job of programming also had to be made easier. Flipping switches and rearranging the hardware took too much time and allowed too many errors. Even before they had finished the ENIAC, Mauchly and Eckert were already making important decisions about their next computer; Eckert had started to design improvements as early as January

For eight years, the army used the ENIAC to calculate ballistics tables, work on problems related to the hydrogen bomb, and help with wind tunnel design. The machine was retired in 1955.

In 1932, John Mauchly had married Mary Augusta Walzl, a mathematician, with whom he had two children. On September 8, 1946, Mary accidentally drowned while she and John were swimming together in the ocean. Two years later, he married Kathleen McNulty, one of the ENIAC programmers. Pres Eckert also experienced tragedy in his personal life; in 1953, his wife of 10 years, Hester Caldwell, committed suicide.

1944. His most important idea was to change the programming technique from a mechanical process to an entirely electronic one. The program would be stored in the computer's memory, where it was easy to input and change. He even designed memory circuits for this, based on some early radar work he had done for the Moore School several years earlier.

In the summer of 1944, a chance meeting between Herman Goldstine, the army officer who oversaw the Moore School's trajectory project, and John von Neumann, a world-famous mathematician, began a chain of events that would have a profound impact on Eckert and Mauchly's work. Goldstine, a mathematician himself, met von Neumann while they were both waiting for the same train. Well acquainted with von Neumann's work and perhaps more than a little in awe of the man, Goldstine started to tell him about the exciting project he was involved in at the Moore School. Von Neumann was interested because, unknown to Goldstine, he was involved with a top-secret government project in Los Alamos, New Mexico, to develop the world's first atomic weapon. This involved a mind-numbing number of calculations, and the ENIAC sounded like just the thing he needed. He began to make regular visits to the Moore School to keep track of developments on the ENIAC. He also had numerous discussions with Goldstine and Eckert about the designs for their next computer. Eckert independently designed most of the key improvements, but von Neumann's input served to make them more clear and practical.

By the time the ENIAC was completed in 1945, the Moore School was already negotiating with the army for funding to build Mauchly and Eckert's next computer, the Electronic Discrete Variable Automatic Computer (EDVAC). Sometime in early 1945, von Neumann wrote the first draft of a paper summarizing many of the project's proposed innovations, offering his own commentary and opinions on them. He gave it to Goldstine to type up into a memo for the rest of the project team. In June, Goldstine produced a 101-page document entitled "First Draft of a Report on the EDVAC." For some reason, Goldstine listed von Neumann as the sole author, although many of the ideas he discussed came from the ENIAC team even before von Neumann became aware of the project. Since the document was intended only for other project members, this didn't seem like much of a problem. Goldstine, however, sent 24 copies of the paper to von Neumann's colleagues at universities in the U.S. and England. It was well received, and requests poured in for more copies. The paper became one of the most important documents in the history of computers, and von Neumann was credited with its ideas. The error continues even to this day: most books list von Neumann as the "real" inventor of the modern computer.

The battle for recognition was not the only battle Eckert and Mauchly faced. With the ENIAC completed, the Moore School began to see dollar signs. Although the pair's contract with the school assigned them exclusive patent rights to the ENIAC

From 1933 until his death, John von Neumann (1903-1957) did brilliant work in mathematics at Princeton University's Institute for Advanced Study (IAS). He also made notable contributions to computer science, especially in seeing how computers could be applied to problem-solving in all scientific fields. Von Neumann was falsely credited with creating the EDVAC, but he did develop a high-speed stored-program electronic digital computer for the IAS. Completed in 1952, this machine served as the model for IBM's first fully electronic stored-program computer, the 701.

patent: government recognition that an invention belongs to a particular inventor, which gives the inventor the sole right to produce and sell the invention for the duration of the patent

In November 1952, Columbia Broadcasting System (CBS) used the UNIVAC to predict the outcome of the presidential election. In a highly publicized marketing gimmick, UNIVAC programmers fed in the results from the first polls to close on election night. Although human analysts expected a close race, the UNIVAC predicted a landslide victory for Dwight Eisenhower. CBS decided that the machine was wrong and produced a fake "report" from the computer showing a more closely contested race. But when the final reports came in, the original prediction turned out to have been a mere four percent different than the actual results! CBS admitted on the air what it had done, and the UNIVAC became an instant celebrity.

and all its components, the design work they did for the EDVAC was not covered under any formal agreement. The university tried to force Eckert and Mauchly to sign away their patent rights to the EDVAC work. Just five weeks after the ENIAC's wildly successful debut, Eckert and Mauchly resigned from their posts in protest.

The duo decided that it would be in their best interest to stick together. Believing computer technology could advance faster in the world of business and government than in academia, in September 1946 they signed a contract to build a computer for the U.S. Bureau of Standards. Orders from other agencies soon followed, and in October, Mauchly and Eckert started the world's first computer company. Originally called the Electronic Control Company, it was incorporated in December 1947 as the Eckert-Mauchly Computer Corporation. Its first job was to develop an improved EDVAC to sell to its clients. Building the EDVAC II, later renamed the Universal Automatic Computer (UNIVAC), proved difficult and expensive, however. Mauchly and Eckert struggled to complete the project until 1950, when they sold their troubled business to Remington Rand, a typewriter company that wanted to move into the computer market. The UNIVAC was completed by Remington Rand in March 1951. It had just 5,000 vacuum tubes and a brand-new magnetic tape input system that was vastly more efficient than punch cards.

Although Eckert and Mauchly never received the recognition they deserved for their inventions, both continued to work with computers for the rest of their lives. Eckert remained with Remington Rand through several name changes, takeovers, and mergers, eventually becoming a corporate vice president. In 1989, he retired from Unisys, as the company was then called. As for Mauchly, he left the company in 1959 to form Mauchly Associates, the first of several new businesses he would start. None was very successful, so in 1973, he rejoined the company he left, then called Sperry, as a consultant.

John Mauchly died on January 8, 1980, during heart surgery at Abington Hospital in Pennsylvania. Eckert lived for several more years, immersing himself in private electronics projects and advocating the use of increasingly smaller, more personal computers, until his death from leukemia on June 3, 1995.

Left to right: An unidentified technician, Pres Eckert, and CBS reporter Walter Cronkite with the UNIVAC during the 1952 election publicity stunt. Remington Rand produced a total of 46 UNIVAC systems, and they remained in use by government agencies and businesses through the 1960s.

CHAPTER FOUR

Jack Kilby and Robert Noyce and the Integrated Circuit

A little bit of Jack Kilby is in your pocket. On your wrist, there's a small piece of Robert Noyce. When you turn on your television or boot up your computer, something of both Kilby and Noyce is inside. Of course, it isn't the men themselves in your calculator, watch, TV, and computer, but it's their invention. These two men, as engineers at competing electronics companies, invented the integrated circuit (often called a microchip) that makes almost everything possible in modern electronics, especially computers.

Jack St. Clair Kilby was born on November 8, 1923, in Jefferson City, Missouri, and he grew up in Kansas. Strangely, it was a snowstorm that sparked his early interest in electronics. In April 1938, an intense blizzard knocked out power and telephone lines across Kansas. Jack's father, Hubert, was the president of the Kansas Power Company in Great Bend, which supplied power for much of the western

Jack Kilby (top; b. 1923) and Robert Noyce (1927-1990) illustrate a very important principle of invention: that two talented individuals may come up with the same idea at around the same time, independently of each other.

circuit: a collection of components through which electricity flows

semiconductor: a class of materials whose ability to conduct electricity lies between that of good insulators (such as rubber) and powerful conductors (such as copper). Semiconductors conduct electricity under certain circumstances, such as when impurities are added to them.

part of the state. During the crisis, Hubert Kilby enlisted local amateur ("ham") radio operators to help him communicate with his power plants. Watching the radio operators, young Jack was fascinated by their ability to pick signals out of the air and turn them into human contacts. Soon, Jack was taking his amateur radio license exam and building his own radio. He later credited ham radio, and especially the blizzard of 1938, with launching him on the path to a career in electronics.

Jack Kilby applied to only one college: the Massachusetts Institute of Technology (MIT). When he failed the entrance exam by three points, though, a bit of last-minute wrangling got him into the University of Illinois. Soon after he started college in 1941, the United States entered World War II and Kilby joined the U.S. Army. He spent the war repairing radios in India, then returned to Illinois to study electrical engineering. There, Kilby learned to create circuits using vacuum tubes, the best electrical switches and signal amplifiers of the day. He graduated in 1947—shortly before Bell Labs introduced a new technology that would make much of his training obsolete.

Invented in 1947 by Bell engineers William Shockley, Walter Brattain, and John Bardeen, the transistor was a replacement for vacuum tubes. It was made of semiconductor material, which conducted electricity only under certain circumstances. That quality made semiconductors ideal for controlling the flow of electricity through a circuit. A transistor consisted of a layer of positively charged

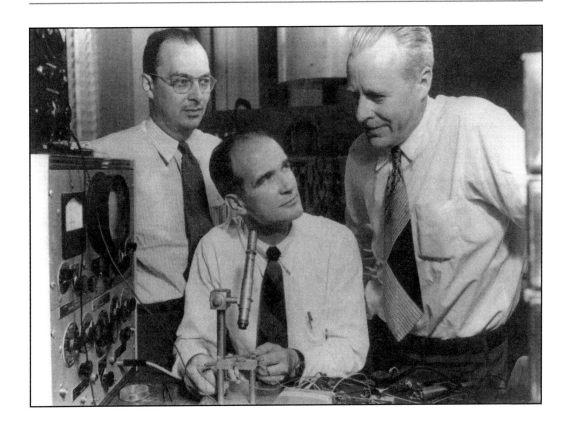

semiconductor material sandwiched between two layers of negatively charged semiconductor material. The input wire from an electrical circuit was attached to one of the outer layers of the transistor, and the output wire was attached to the other outer layer. The middle layer acted as an insulator, refusing to allow electricity to pass through the circuit. When electricity was applied to the middle layer, though, it would become conductive and allow electrons to pass from the input side to the output side. Thus, the middle layer could act as a switch, controlling the flow of electricity through the circuit.

Left to right: John Bardeen, William Shockley, and Walter Brattain in 1948, with the equipment they used to develop the transistor. The three men won the Nobel Prize in physics for their invention.

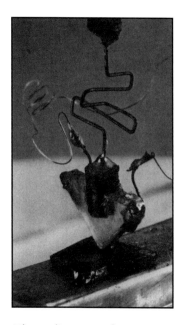

The rudimentary first transistor, known as a point-contact transistor, was simply a slab of germanium and a plastic triangle coated in gold foil. The gold at the tip of the triangle was cut in half so that it touched the germanium at two separate points. Electricity entered the germanium at one point and exited, amplified, at the other. By 1951, William Shockley and his Bell Labs team had improved upon this design, creating the junction transistor, in which two layers of negatively charged semiconductor material surrounded a positively charged layer.

Transistors enjoyed almost every advantage over vacuum tubes. Vacuum tubes consumed large amounts of energy, generated a lot of heat, and often burned out (just like their cousins, light bulbs). Transistors used less energy, produced less heat, did not burn out, and lasted longer. They could also switch on and off at least 12 times faster than vacuum tubes. And while a vacuum tube might be the size of an egg or larger, the first transistors were about the size of pencil erasers. All this meant that electronics made with transistors could be smaller, cheaper, and more reliable than ever before. In the 1940s, radios using vacuum tubes had been so big that they were housed in large cabinets; the first transistor radio, which debuted in 1954, was pocket-sized. Within just a few years, transistors made designs based on vacuum tubes obsolete.

One of the engineers who quickly saw the transistor's potential was Robert Noyce. The son of a Congregationalist minister, Robert was born on December 12, 1927, in Burlington, Iowa. As a young boy, he once lost a model airplane because the engine he built for it was too powerful—it just kept flying until it was out of sight. To ensure that never happened again, for his next airplane he designed and built a radio-control unit. Robert earned money to finance his model planes and other hobbies by mowing lawns. One of his customers was Professor Grant Gale, chairman of the physics department at Grinnell College. Under Gale's tutelage, high-school-aged Robert Noyce studied college-level math and physics. In 1945, Noyce enrolled at Grinnell, where he majored in physics.

Grant Gale was a friend of John Bardeen, one of the inventors of the transistor. Through Bardeen, Gale obtained one of the first transistors and showed it to his students. Noyce immediately recognized it as a revolutionary device and studied everything he could about it. By 1948, when he entered MIT to get his Ph.D. in physics, he knew more about transistors than some of his professors did.

After graduating from MIT in 1953, Noyce worked making transistors at Philco, a Philadelphia electronics company. The scientific papers he wrote caught the eye of William Shockley, another co-inventor of the transistor. In 1956, Shockley invited Noyce to join him and others in starting a new company in California, Shockley Semiconductor Laboratories. Noyce jumped at the chance, but he soon grew disappointed with the brilliant engineer's poor management. By early 1957, Noyce and seven others left the company. Backed by a large investment from Fairchild Camera and Instrument Company, the men started Fairchild Semiconductor to produce their own transistors. At just 29 years old, Noyce became general manager of the company.

Meanwhile, Jack Kilby had spent 10 years working for Centralab, a Milwaukee-based company that made parts for radios, televisions, and hearing aids—all of which used high-quality amplifiers. In 1952, Bell Labs announced that it would issue licenses to companies that wanted to manufacture transistors. Centralab paid the license fee and sent

In the early 1950s, transistors began to be put to innovative uses. Texas Instruments created the first commercial transistor radio, the Regency, in 1954; other companies soon produced their own models, and business boomed. Coinciding with the rise of rock 'n' roll music, transistor radios proved very popular with young people, who liked being able to listen to music wherever they wanted and (because many transistor radios came with headphones) as loudly as they wanted. Thanks to the transistor, radio sets went from being pieces of furniture shared by entire families to personal accessories owned by individuals.

Working at Centralab from 1947 to 1958, Kilby produced 12 patentable inventions. During that time, he also took evening classes at the University of Wisconsin, earning his master's degree in electrical engineering in 1950.

Kilby to a 10-day Bell crash course to learn all he could about how to use transistors. He soon realized what engineers everywhere were finding out: the transistor's size was one of its greatest strengths, but it was also a weakness. On paper, engineers could draw complicated circuit diagrams calling for thousands of transistors and other components. But building such devices was another matter. The more components were added to a circuit, the more connections needed to be made between them. Hand-soldering 10 or 20 tiny wires to each component was expensive, time-consuming, and unreliable— plus, each extra wire meant the electricity had to travel farther and the circuit would become slower. Beyond a certain point, adding components became virtually impossible. This limitation prevented a wide variety of new devices, already designed on paper, from being built. Engineers invented a new term, "the tyranny of numbers," to describe the phenomenon, and solving the tyranny of numbers became one of the top priorities of the day.

Kilby was determined to find a cost-effective, reliable way to produce and interconnect circuit components, but the resources at Centralab weren't enough. In 1958, he began to look for another position. When a relative newcomer in the electronics field, Texas Instruments (TI), offered Kilby a job specifically trying to solve the tyranny of numbers problem, he accepted. In May 1958, around the same time that Robert Noyce helped found Fairchild Semiconductor, Jack Kilby moved to Dallas with his wife, Barbara, and their two young daughters.

THE BREAKTHROUGH

Just a few weeks after he arrived at TI, Kilby found himself virtually alone in the lab. TI encouraged all its employees to take their summer vacations simultaneously during two weeks in July, but Kilby didn't have any vacation time saved up yet. He took advantage of his temporary freedom.

Kilby started by plowing through piles of technical literature until he understood the problem of the tyranny of numbers from every angle. He knew there are four basic components that control the flow of electricity in every circuit: transistors, resistors, diodes, and capacitors. A resistor "resists" the electrical current, slowing the electrons down and making it more difficult for them to pass through. A diode acts like a one-way gate, keeping electricity flowing in the same direction around the circuit. A capacitor is like a small battery that soaks up an electrical charge and releases it later, either all at once (like the circuitry that powers the flash in a camera) or gradually. By combining these parts in various ways, one could make an unlimited number of devices.

Transistors at the time were typically made of an element called germanium. Germanium was easy to work with, but it had a serious drawback: it didn't operate well at high temperatures. In 1954, TI had figured out how to make transistors from silicon, an element that was much more difficult to work with but didn't suffer germanium's heat sensitivity. Silicon diodes were widely available, too. Kilby thought that it would also be possible to build resistors and

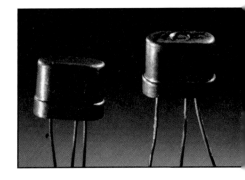

Texas Instruments produced the first commercial silicon transistors.

capacitors from silicon. That led to what has been termed his "monolithic idea": if all individual components could be made of the same material (silicon), it should be possible to create them all from a single piece of that material. If a single piece of silicon could be manufactured with all the components already embedded in it, it would be simple to lay out the circuit's connections. The resistors, diodes, capacitors, and transistors would come preconnected—users could just plug in the whole circuit and go. Since all the components for a circuit would be integrated on the same chip of silicon, Kilby's invention is called the integrated circuit (IC).

When everyone returned from vacation, Kilby convinced his boss, Willis Adcock, to let him build a prototype. Kilby started small: first he attempted to make capacitors and resistors from silicon. When he succeeded, he tried building all four types of components on the same silicon wafer. Kilby made it by hand, connecting the components using thin gold wires and a magnifying glass. The chip was only 1.5 centimeters long and a few millimeters wide; to keep from losing it, he glued it to a glass microscope slide. On September 12, 1958, fellow engineers and TI executives crowded into Kilby's corner of the lab to see if his radical new concept would work. Luck was with him; it worked the first time. But Kilby still had a problem: he had no idea how to manufacture all the interconnections needed to make the microchip practical. That's where Robert Noyce came in.

Fairchild Semiconductor was founded to manufacture a new type of silicon transistor known as a

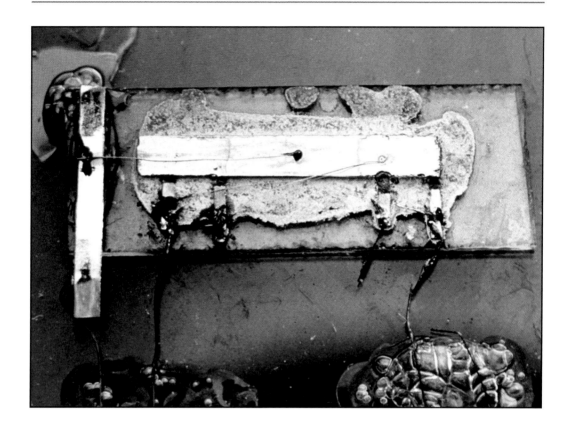

double diffusion transistor. This device turned out to be highly susceptible to failure because dirt, dust, tiny electrical charges at the wrong locations, or any of a number of other things could easily ruin it. One of Fairchild's engineers suggested encasing the transistor in a thin coating of silicon oxide, which would protect it from contamination. Noyce noticed that the layer also provided a convenient anchor for the wires connecting the transistor to a circuit. Then he realized that the wires would be unnecessary if electrical pathways—tiny lines of copper or another metal—could be printed right on the silicon oxide.

Jack Kilby's prototype of the integrated circuit

Robert Noyce's innovation eventually brought Fairchild Semiconductor great success. In 1963, Noyce (third from left) posed with other Fairchild executives at the opening of the company's new manufacturing plant in South Portland, Maine. Forty years later, the facility continued to produce integrated circuits.

Printing was much cheaper, faster, and more reliable than connecting a wire that could come loose.

Noyce also expanded his ideas beyond transistors, inventing the same sort of silicon resistors and capacitors Kilby had made just a few months before. On January 23, 1959, Noyce filled up four pages of his lab notebook with basically the world's second description of an integrated circuit. He had independently reached the same solution that Kilby had, but while Kilby hadn't worked out how to make the interconnections, Noyce had. Although Kilby's design was first, Noyce's was the first practical solution that could be mass produced.

THE RESULT

A few days after Noyce wrote his description of an integrated circuit, a rumor circulated at Texas Instruments that RCA, a competitor, was developing an IC. This was false, but TI's executives decided to apply for a patent on Kilby's invention—in a hurry. TI filed its application on February 6, 1959.

A patent application must include full details and drawings of the device being patented. But Kilby still didn't know a practical way to make the interconnections, so his application included a diagram of his prototype handmade chip with fine gold wires connecting the components. He knew his "flying wire diagram" wasn't the right solution, but it was the best he could do at the time. Kilby did have a vague idea, though, and it was remarkably similar to Noyce's. He inserted a paragraph into the application speculating that instead of wires, one could apply a layer of silicon oxide and "lay down" gold circuitry on top. Still, he had never done it, and he did not know if it would work.

Someone at Fairchild Semiconductor heard that TI was about to announce an IC. It was only then that Noyce mentioned his idea to anyone besides his immediate colleagues. In July 1959, several months after TI, Fairchild filed its own patent application—and somehow, Fairchild's patent application was processed first. In April 1961, Noyce was granted U.S. patent #2,981,877. Since patents are awarded only to the original inventor, TI challenged Noyce's award, and in May 1962 their case,

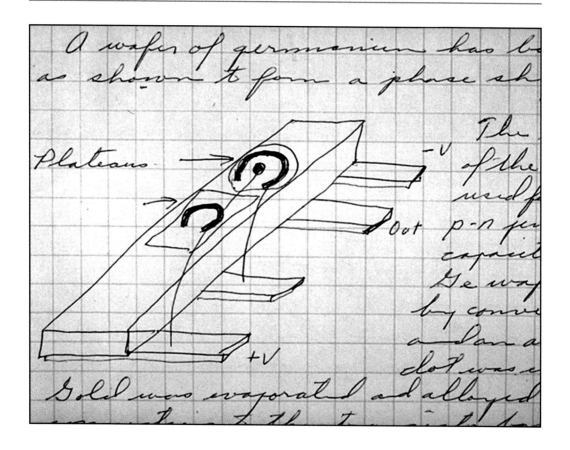

Kilby's "flying wire" diagram of the integrated circuit

Kilby v. Noyce, went before the Board of Patent Interferences. While the legal battle geared up, Kilby's patent was also granted.

Both Kilby and Noyce had kept detailed lab notebooks containing descriptions of their work and, importantly, the dates on which it was performed. Kilby was able to show that he conceived of the monolithic idea six months before Noyce. But Noyce's application detailed exactly how to construct the interconnections, and Kilby's did not. Five years later, on February 24, 1967, the board issued its opinion in Kilby's favor. Fairchild appealed, and in November, the Court of Customs and Patent Appeals awarded the patent to Noyce. TI filed an appeal with the U.S. Supreme Court, which refused to hear the case. So *Kilby v. Noyce* ended with Noyce declared the inventor of the IC.

Fortunately for the world, the two companies didn't leave the matter entirely to their lawyers. In the summer of 1966, TI and Fairchild decided to cross-license: TI granted Fairchild the right to use whatever IC technology it currently had, as well as any future developments, and Fairchild granted TI the same rights. That cleared the way for both companies to produce the chips, knowing each was protected from the other however the case turned out. (Cross-licensing also required any other companies that wanted to make integrated circuits to pay royalties to both TI and Fairchild.)

The first ICs were expensive, costing about $120 apiece, and the electronics industry viewed them with suspicion. It was the U.S. government that became the first and largest consumer of ICs, buying millions per year for its science and defense programs. The U.S. military used them in the Minuteman II missile, while the National Aeronautics and Space Administration (NASA) used them in flight computers for the Apollo space program, which eventually landed the first human on the Moon in 1969. Soon, however, engineers were finding new uses for ICs in dozens of other industries. The first commercial use of an IC was in a

Texas Instruments' electronic handheld calculator was invented by Jack Kilby, Jerry Merryman, and James Van Tassel. Although it measured only about six inches tall, four inches wide, and two inches thick, it was as powerful as much larger machines. TI went on to dominate the calculator market.

Zenith hearing aid in 1964, and in the 1970s the semiconductor business really took off.

Both Kilby and Noyce continued to work in the electronics industry. In 1968, Noyce and his coworker Gordon Moore started a company to design and manufacture new kinds of ICs. They named their company "Intel," playing on the words "integrated electronics" and "intelligence." Intel's engineers went on to invent the microprocessor, an extremely complex IC, versions of which serve as central processing units in almost every computer today. Kilby stayed on at TI, where he headed teams that built the first military systems and the first computer to incorporate ICs. In 1967, he also used ICs to create the world's first handheld electric calculator. Although he officially retired from the company in the 1980s, he remained involved as a consultant.

Both Kilby and Noyce were honored many times for their pivotal roles in advancing electronics technology. And remarkably, considering the long legal battle, neither man harbored any resentment toward the other. In 1969, Kilby received the National Medal of Science, which Noyce also received in 1979. In 1982, Kilby was inducted into the National Inventors' Hall of Fame, an honor Noyce received the following year. Noyce died of a heart attack in June 1990; his death left only Kilby eligible for the nomination for the Nobel Prize in physics, which he won in 2000. In his acceptance speech, Kilby graciously pointed out that Noyce also deserved credit for the IC.

By that time, the integrated circuit Kilby and Noyce developed was worth an estimated $177 billion a year worldwide. The market for all electronic devices that depended on ICs was almost $1.2 trillion. Today, virtually every electronic device requires at least one integrated circuit, often many. Next time you look at your digital watch, use your calculator, turn on your television, or boot up your computer, you can thank Jack Kilby and Robert Noyce, two men who dreamed up the same solution at almost the same time.

Jack Kilby poses with some of the many products that use integrated circuits.

CHAPTER FIVE

Ted Hoff
and the Microprocessor

"Announcing a new era of integrated electronics: a microprogrammable computer on a chip." That's how the Intel Development Corporation's advertisement read in the November 15, 1971, issue of *Electronic News* magazine. Most ads for new products tend to inflate their importance, but Intel's grandiose wording actually underestimated the eventual impact of its innovation. The product was known simply by a number, 4004, but despite this mundane name, it would change the world forever. The Intel 4004 was the world's first microprocessor, the "brain" of a modern computer. Even its inventor, Ted Hoff, could hardly have imagined the effect it would have on the everyday lives of billions of people.

Marcian Edward Hoff was born on October 28, 1937, in Rochester, New York. He grew up outside Rochester, near a small village called North Chili, where he attended a one-room schoolhouse with just 13 students. Ted (as he liked to be called) didn't

Ted Hoff (b. 1937) helped transform the Intel Corporation into a giant of the computing industry by creating a tiny chip that could run an entire computer.

rely solely on school for his education, however. His father worked for the General Railway Signal Company, which made devices to help coordinate the traffic flow of trains. From his father, Ted learned to work with electricity. He also developed an interest in chemistry when an uncle showed him how two colorless liquids could combine to make a solution that was bright red. He studied on his own, and even though he never took a high-school chemistry course, he passed the New York State chemistry exam with a score of 95 out of 100.

Ted's uncle steered him away from chemistry as a career choice, since he knew that jobs were scarce. Instead, he gave Ted a subscription to *Popular Science* magazine, a hobbyist publication with a strong electronics slant; sure enough, Ted's interest shifted. In 1954, he enrolled at Rensselaer Polytechnic Institute, where he received a bachelor's degree in electrical engineering in 1958. During summers, he worked as a lab technician, designing track circuits at the General Railway Signal Company. Despite his young age, Ted Hoff's contributions were so valuable that he was listed on two patents as a co-inventor.

After finishing at Rensselaer, Hoff moved to California and enrolled in graduate engineering courses at Stanford University. He received his master's degree in 1959 and his Ph.D. in 1962, then stayed on at Stanford as a researcher. One of his projects involved a new type of computer memory, and this experience led to a job with a new semiconductor company called Intel. On September 1, 1968, Hoff became Intel's 12th employee.

One of Ted's classmates once worked for a whole weekend to solve an engineering homework assignment. "I ran into Ted at about 11 and asked if he had done it," the classmate remembered. "'No,' was his answer, 'not yet.' But in class, less than two hours later, he had finished it."

Intel's main business was developing computer memory chips, and Hoff's job was to find new uses for these products so Intel could sell more of them to different markets. After just a few months in his new job, Hoff was asked to work with a group of engineers from Busicom, a Japanese company that made electronic calculators. Busicom wanted Intel to produce a set of integrated circuit chips for a new line of high-performance desktop calculators. The plans called for 12 different custom-designed chips that would need as many as 3,000 transistors each—at a time when typical integrated circuits used just 500 to 1,000. Such complex chips would be difficult for Intel's small staff to design, hard to manufacture, and costly to both companies. After a little thought, Hoff came up with a better idea.

Intel was founded by Robert Noyce and Gordon Moore on July 18, 1968, in Mountain View, California. The memory chips it manufactured were special types of integrated circuits (ICs) that could store information.

THE BREAKTHROUGH

Busicom's proposed design irked Ted Hoff. The production cost was so high the calculator's eventual price would be near that of a much more powerful minicomputer.

Minicomputers were state-of-the-art in 1969. Ranging from the size of a trunk to the size of a large desk, they were a popular way to provide low-cost computing. For a few thousand dollars, they could be programmed to do just about anything, from simple arithmetic to complex scientific calculations. Some bored young programmers had even written games for minicomputers, like the popular Spacewar, the first video game.

A calculator, on the other hand, could only do arithmetic. Hoff felt it would be silly to expect people to pay for such a limited device when just as much money would buy them a multipurpose computer. Intel's marketing department disagreed, pointing out that, as an engineer, of course Hoff would opt for the minicomputer. But most people weren't engineers, and they wouldn't want to go through the trouble of starting up a computer and programming it to solve their problems when they could just punch a few keys on the calculator. It might be less versatile, Intel's marketers argued, but a calculator was enormously easier to use.

This argument failed to satisfy Hoff. As long as Intel was going to the massive effort to produce the calculator chips, it might as well produce something that could be used not just for calculators, but

minicomputer: a mid-sized computer, smaller than a mainframe (a large, powerful computer that often has multiple terminals) but larger than a personal computer

for a variety of other things too. The chips Busicom had planned would need many different circuits for each type of operation they would perform. Each circuit was specialized, so it could only do the same job over and over again. In technical terms, this was known as hard-wired logic because the wiring and components were fixed in place at the time of manufacturing. The circuits could do only what they were designed to—nothing else.

Hoff decided that the calculator really needed a programmable chip, which later became known as a microprocessor. At the time, computers had different chips for each task—one chip might read user input, another perform various mathematic functions, and a third store results. Hoff's design would integrate most of these different chips into a single chip, a version of a computer's central processing unit (CPU). Such a chip could perform a variety of tasks, depending on what it was asked to do. An engineer could write a very detailed set of low-level instructions, called a program, and place it in a memory chip. Both this memory chip and the microprocessor chip would be wired into the same circuit. The microprocessor would read its instructions from the memory chip, and by writing different instructions, engineers could make the processor perform many roles. Creating such a general-purpose chip would be a challenge, Hoff knew, but so would designing the custom-made, super-dense integrated circuits that Busicom's plan called for. The difference was that once the microprocessor was completed, the individual chips could be made more

central processing unit (CPU): the part of a computer that interprets and carries out instructions

cheaply. They could also be used for other things besides calculators, so the initial high cost of development could be offset by selling more chips.

When Hoff presented his idea to Busicom engineers, they were not impressed. They didn't see any need to create a general-purpose computer chip when hard-wired logic would do. But Robert Noyce, Intel's president and cofounder, saw the idea's merit and encouraged Hoff to proceed. Hoff and another Intel engineer, Stanley Mazor, started to design the new programmable integrated circuit. They had to figure out what functions it would need, decide how it would interact with the other parts of the device, and determine the electrical specifications. Actually producing a chip would be expensive, so that was left for later, after they had a commitment from Busicom.

Robert Noyce (center) and Gordon Moore (right) had founded Intel after growing frustrated with the management at their previous company, Fairchild Semiconductor (where Noyce had invented the integrated circuit in 1958). Despite having no prior management experience, they made Intel a success. Andrew Grove (left), head of production while Hoff was working on the Busicom chips, went on to lead the company in the 1980s and 1990s.

In October 1969, Hoff again met with Busicom engineers. This time, having worked things through on paper, he was able to present a more detailed proposal, which Busicom accepted. Busicom agreed to pay Intel $60,000 to produce the chips, and in return Intel gave Busicom exclusive rights to use them. Hoff was relieved that the project was going to proceed. He and Mazor had worked out a good design for what they called the 4004. But they needed a specialist to turn the design into an actual blueprint to be etched onto a chip and manufactured. Shortly thereafter, Intel hired Federico Faggin, a talented chip designer from Italy who had been working at another Silicon Valley company.

Faggin's first assignment was to build the 4004 based on Hoff and Mazor's plan. One of Busicom's engineers was due soon to approve the final chip design. Unfortunately, it was anything but finished. Since no one had ever made a microprocessor before, Faggin found himself having to invent new ways of implementing the design in silicon. Faggin, Mazor, and the Busicom engineer, Masatoshi Shima, worked furiously, often putting in 12-to-16-hour days. They finally completed their task, and in February 1971, Faggin delivered to Busicom several completed 4004 chips, along with eight other chips necessary to make the calculator work. The Intel 4004 was only 1/8 inch long by 1/6 inch wide, and it included about 2,300 transistors. It fit easily on even the smallest fingernail, yet it equaled the performance of computers that, just five years earlier, had been the size of a large desk.

Most electronic chips are made from the element silicon. Northern California, specifically the area south of San Francisco, is known for its extremely high concentration of electronics and computer companies, both of which use a lot of chips—earning that area the nickname "Silicon Valley." Besides Intel, companies located in the area include Apple Computer, Hewlett-Packard, Pixar, and Xerox.

The Intel 4004 chip shown much larger than its fingertip size (left). A magnified view of the interior (right) reveals the intricate electrical pathways.

THE RESULT

Although the 4004 was a huge leap forward, Intel's contract with Busicom prevented microprocessors from being sold to anyone else. Unfortunately for Busicom, its calculator business wasn't doing well. By 1971, it was in deep financial trouble and facing bankruptcy. It approached Intel seeking to pay a lower price for 4004 chips. Hoff persuaded his superiors that Intel should try to get back the rights to the chip, so the company offered to return Busicom's initial investment in exchange for permission to sell the 4004 to other customers. Busicom gladly agreed.

Now that Intel had the right to sell the 4004, however, the marketing department was unwilling to try. Intel's main business was marketing relatively simple memory chips; it sold caseloads of them to manufacturers along with simple schematics that told engineers how to make their circuits work with Intel chips. But selling the 4004 was different. First of all, the product was so unlike anything else that it required a lot of marketing (and money) to help customers understand just how much the product could do for them. Second, the 4004 wasn't as easy to use as a memory chip. Customers would have to learn to produce an entire computer around the chip, and then program for it. Intel would need to supply a mountain of technical handbooks, and producing such documentation was arduous and expensive. The company would also have to provide some sort of customer support, both to give sample designs around which customers could base their own, and to answer questions from the customers' engineers. In all, selling the 4004 seemed a monumental task. The worldwide market for minicomputers was only about 20,000 per year, and Intel could expect to make only a fraction of those sales. The marketing department decided Hoff's new invention just wasn't worth all the trouble and cost.

But Hoff was persistent. No one knew what to do with the unique chips yet, but that didn't mean Intel couldn't show them. Hoff argued that, using the 4004, engineers could design circuits with fewer chips. The money saved would more than pay for the expense of redesigning the circuit around an Intel CPU chip. The chip's extremely small size also meant that it could be embedded in devices that had never before been computerized, such as gas pumps, traffic signals, and elevator control systems. Hoff's persistence paid off, and Intel ran the first ad promoting its new CPU in fall 1971. Adam Osborne, one of the company's engineers, was given the task of organizing all the documentation that customers would need to use the chip. Customers gradually began to realize that the microprocessor could be a cheap, compact, and versatile central control system for a wide variety of devices, especially computers.

Intel's first advertisement for the 4004, which ran in the magazine Electronic News

Hoff later commented that proving a market existed for the microprocessor was almost a greater accomplishment than inventing it in the first place. He had demonstrated "that the computer, a little chunk of intelligence, was a very marketable building block."

Demand for Intel's microprocessors grew steadily. In 1974, it introduced a newer, more powerful model, the Intel 8080. The 8080's design incorporated 4,500 transistors, almost double the number of the 4004. Where the 4004 could execute 60,000 instructions every second, the 8080 could manage 290,000. By then, competitors had begun producing microprocessors, such as Motorola's 6800 chip. The 8080 beat them out, however, quickly becoming an industry standard. Four years later, Intel introduced an improved high-end version, the 8086, and a less expensive model, the 8088, which used the same set of instructions, so programs written for one also ran on the other. In 1981, when IBM announced its first personal computer (PC), it used the Intel 8088 CPU. Newer PC models from IBM continued to use 8086-compatible CPUs.

Although Intel started as a memory company, it became best known as the manufacturer of newer, more powerful chips in the 8086 family, including the 80186, 80286, 80386, 80486, Pentium, Pentium II, Pentium Pro, Pentium III, Pentium 4, and others. Other companies, most notably Advanced Micro Devices (AMD), also began manufacturing 8086-compatible CPUs. By 2003, the microprocessor was the most complex mass-produced product ever, with more than 5.5 million transistors performing

Adam Osborne went on to found his own technical publishing house, putting out an extensive array of computer manuals for all kinds of software and hardware. He later founded the Osborne Computer Corporation, which introduced the first commercially successful portable computer, the Osborne I, in 1981.

Intel continued to improve upon Hoff's creation. The Pentium Processor, introduced in 1993, was 1,500 times faster than the 4004, and subsequent chips kept getting faster.

Within a few years of its introduction, the IBM PC became the industry standard for personal computers—and its Intel CPU became the industry standard for microprocessors.

billions of calculations every second. The worldwide market for microprocessors and devices that used microprocessors was estimated at about $500 billion.

In 1983, Hoff left Intel to become a vice president at Atari, the leading manufacturer of video games and video-game consoles. When Atari was sold in 1984, Hoff and his coworker Gary Summers decided to open a consulting business. They founded Teklicon, a firm that provided technical expertise to law firms on intellectual property cases. Hoff was the vice president and chief technologist. At home, he enjoyed tinkering around in his own fully equipped electronics lab, which included a small machine shop for making mechanical parts. Hoff was repeatedly honored for his revolutionary invention. In 1996, he, Faggin, and Mazor were inducted into the National Inventors' Hall of Fame. In 2000, they each received the Semiconductor Industry Association's highest honor, the Robert N. Noyce Award, which was named for the co-inventor of the microchip and Hoff's former boss.

Left to right: Ted Hoff, Federico Faggin, and Stanley Mazor at the time of their induction into the National Inventors' Hall of Fame.

CHAPTER SIX

Steve Wozniak and the Personal Computer

Stanley Zebrezuskinitski told jokes. In 1974, one of San Francisco's most popular phone numbers was his Dial-a-Joke service. Although the jokes were usually recorded on an answering machine, sometimes he liked to pick up the phone and play sly tricks on his callers. "I bet I can hang up faster than you!" he told a woman named Alice Robertson. She must have had a sense of humor, because she later married him. Of course, his name wasn't Stanley Zebrezuskinitski, and his contribution to the field of computing was no laughing matter. His real name was Steve Wozniak, or as he liked to be called, "The Woz," and he invented the personal computer.

Stephen Gary Wozniak was born on August 11, 1950, in San Jose, California. His engineer father, Jerry, always encouraged Steve's interest in science, math, and electronics. "My dad got local transistor companies . . . to donate 'cosmetic defects' of hundreds of diodes and transistors to me," Steve recalled.

Stephen Gary Wozniak (b.1950) invented the personal computer, an easy-to-use machine that has changed the way people work, learn, play, shop, and talk to each other.

Steve Wozniak was often quiet and shy, but he was also a prankster. In high school, he built a device that could set off fire alarms. He had another device that could jam the frequency on a TV, making the picture go haywire and causing unsuspecting viewers—like his younger sister and brother, Leslie and Mark—to try to adjust the antenna. As an adult, he pulled stunts such as reprogramming the telephones at an airport to call his friend's house instead of the local hotels.

Jerry also helped his son understand how they worked. When Steve was in fifth grade, he read a book that inspired him to earn his amateur radio operator's license, and then he built his own transmitter and receiver. The following year, he created a simple computer capable of playing a good game of ticktacktoe.

By the time Steve enrolled in high school in 1964, the electronics and computer industry was growing rapidly in northern California. It employed many of his classmates' parents, and the school offered several electronics classes. Steve took them all, always earned As, and even led the electronics club for two years. The courses, however, weren't much of a challenge for him. Recognizing this, his teacher, John McCollum, arranged for Steve and a classmate to program computers once a week at Sylvania, a nearby electronics company. This was just what Steve needed. He became enthralled with the desk-sized "minicomputers" Sylvania provided. He read all the technical manuals he could, and within weeks he had started sketching designs for his own minicomputer. He papered his bedroom with computer pictures and brochures. At a time when even the smallest computers were much too expensive for any individual, Steve Wozniak resolved that someday he would own one.

In 1968, Wozniak enrolled in the University of Colorado to study engineering. During his first year, he took a graduate-level course in computer programming. He spent long hours in the computer lab writing programs not only for class, but also for his own amusement. He got an A+ in the course, but he used so much computer time that the university wanted to charge him extra for it. He was too scared to tell his parents, so he left the university at the end of his first year. Wozniak moved back to the San Jose area and attended DeAnza Community College for his sophomore year, then took time off to work at a small computer company, Tenet Inc.

In the summer of 1971, Wozniak and a high-school friend named Bill Fernandez got their hands on electronic parts that local companies had labeled unsellable because of scratches or other minor flaws. In less than a week, Wozniak drew a design for a computer they could create from the parts. Fueled by excitement and cream soda, they stayed up all night building what they called their "Cream Soda Computer." The local newspaper even sent a reporter out to see it in action. Unfortunately, as soon as they turned it on, the computer overheated and started to smoke. The reporter was disappointed, but Wozniak was not. He'd had a lot of fun, and to him, that was the important thing.

It was through Bill Fernandez that Wozniak met the man who would have the biggest influence on his career: Steve Jobs. Though Jobs was five years younger, the two shared a passion for technology. Wozniak was a more gifted engineer, but Jobs had unshakable confidence and a clear vision of what he wanted to achieve. The combination of his ambition and Wozniak's skill would prove much more powerful than either man realized at the time.

Steve Wozniak returned to college in 1971, spending his junior year at the University of California in Berkeley. At around the same time, he read a story in *Esquire* magazine based on a man named John Draper, who went by the pseudonym "Captain Crunch." Draper was a "phone phreak"— someone who made a hobby of tricking the phone company's computerized system into doing things it shouldn't, such as giving free long-distance calls. Phreaking was illegal, but Draper and many others viewed it as a fascinating technical challenge. The article described a device called a "little blue box"

Steve Jobs (left) and Steve Wozniak, pictured in 1975, examining a blue box

that Draper used to place free calls. Wozniak decided to try to build one, and it worked. Jobs convinced him to begin selling them to local college students. Wozniak became a fairly well-known phreak himself, under the name "Berkeley Blue."

After a year at Berkeley, Wozniak left school once again, this time for a job working on electronic calculators for the industry giant Hewlett-Packard. In 1975, he joined a group of hobbyists called the Homebrew Computer Club, and for the first time he was surrounded by people who were as passionate and knowledgeable about computers as he was—or even more so. At Homebrew meetings he learned about the Altair, a small computer that could be purchased as a kit and then assembled. Although Wozniak couldn't afford his own Altair, he admired those that other members brought in. He also saw home-built machines similar to his Cream Soda Computer, and he decided he could improve on many of the designs. All he needed was a microprocessor. At the time, however, most were sold only to established companies, and they cost several hundred dollars.

Then Wozniak heard that MOS Technologies would be selling its 6502 microprocessor for only $20 at a computer convention in San Francisco. Although the 6502 chip wasn't as advanced as some others, Wozniak went to the convention and bought one. Soon he had designed and built a computer around the small chip. Like many homemade computers at the time, it was just a circuit board. The user had to wire it to a power supply, a keyboard, and

Draper owed his nickname to a toy whistle from a box of Cap'n Crunch cereal. He discovered that when it was blown into a phone receiver, it would mimic the tones that caused central telephone circuitry to open a long-distance line. His "blue box" sent similar beeping signals. Draper and Wozniak eventually met and became friends; Draper worked briefly for Apple Computer and created a word-processing program called EasyWriter.

The Homebrew Computer Club changed my life. My interest in computers was renewed. Every two weeks the club meeting was the biggest thing in my life.
—Steve Wozniak

The Apple I computer lacked a keyboard and a screen, but in 1976 it was an innovative personal computer.

a television (the screen served as a monitor). Still, it was truly an engineering marvel. Wozniak's design was so simple and elegant that he printed it up on a single sheet of paper and passed it out to Homebrew Club members. The machine was a hit with them.

Steve Jobs dubbed his friend's creation the "Apple." He persuaded Wozniak to start a company with him to produce and sell Apple computers to other hobbyists. Wozniak kept his day job, but on April 1, 1976, the two young men and a colleague, Ron Wayne (who bowed out shortly afterward), founded Apple Computer. Almost immediately, Jobs convinced a local computer store, the Byte Shop, to agree to buy 50 Apple computers. He stretched the company's finances to the limit to afford the new parts they would need, then quickly organized a team to assemble 200 computers within 30 days. Some went to computer stores, while others were sold by mail order from the company's headquarters in Jobs's parents' garage. The retail price was a whimsical $666.66.

The Apple was completely original, and it sold well. The unexpected success enabled the company to attract investors who could provide the money Jobs and Wozniak needed to make Apple Computer a full-time job. Mike Markkula, a retired Intel executive, was so impressed that he bought himself a one-third stake in the company in late 1976. By that time, Wozniak had already begun designing an improved product, the Apple II.

Steve Wozniak, sporting apple-shaped sunglasses, displayed one of his Apple I boards.

THE BREAKTHROUGH

Although the first Apple computer was popular with hobbyists, Wozniak felt he could do better. For one thing, the Apple I (as it was now called, to distinguish it from the Apple II) had been designed to be inexpensive to produce, since Wozniak didn't have a very large budget. Although it was functional, many of the parts didn't offer the performance that he would have liked. For example, the video hardware he had included was capable of writing only 30 characters to the screen each second. This was much faster than the typewriter-like teletype machines that were common at the time, but Wozniak wanted better.

Wozniak also wanted to design a computer that average people—not just computer hobbyists—would want to use. Steve Jobs had worked for Atari, the leading manufacturer of arcade video games, and Wozniak had helped out there with several engineering problems (he even helped design one of the company's most popular early games, Breakout). He knew that people really enjoyed video games, and that games were the limit of most people's exposure to computers. So he decided to make his Apple II the premier home video game system, figuring that once people used his computer for games, they'd use it for other things, too. The Apple I could display only text, but Wozniak designed the Apple II to display high-resolution graphics. Not only that, but it could display them in up to 16 different colors at once, a far cry from the monochrome Apple I. Like the Apple I, though, the Apple II still had to be

The first employee Wozniak and Jobs hired after founding Apple was the friend who had brought them together, Bill Fernandez. Many other employees were drawn from the Homebrew Club, including several still in high school. Youth dominated the company: Jobs was just 21, Wozniak was 26, and even Mike Markkula was only in his 30s, although his Intel stock had already made him a millionaire.

hooked up to a television. But Wozniak added a built-in speaker port so programs could play sounds, and he added ports for controllers called paddles that people could use to play arcade games.

The Apple II used the same central processing unit (CPU) as the Apple I: the MOS Technologies 6502. It had proved quite a capable chip, and it was still much cheaper than its competitors. Just as in computers today, the Apple II's CPU was controlled by a small electronic clock. The clock generated timing pulses to synchronize the operations of all the different parts of the computer, orchestrating them like the conductor of a complex symphony. The speed of the clock was measured in hertz—the number of pulses it generated each second. The CPU in the Apple II ran at 1 million hertz, or 1 megahertz (Mhz), more than fast enough for most games at the time. Wozniak also stuffed the Apple II full of memory. Most other computers came with only 4 kilobytes (K) of random access memory (RAM), but the Apple II's memory could be expanded to up to 48K.

In addition to attracting new users, Wozniak was designing a computer that he himself would like to have. He wanted an easy way to program it to do whatever he required, so he wrote a version of the BASIC programming language. BASIC was very popular among hobbyists because it was easy to learn; complex programs could be written with just a few simple commands. But running programs in BASIC usually involved a lengthy process of loading the language into the memory via cassettes or

Computer memory is measured in bytes. One byte is usually enough memory to store a single letter or small number. 1,024 bytes is called a kilobyte (K or KB). One typewritten page contains about 2K worth of information. 1,024K equals a megabyte (MB), and 1,024MB equals a gigabyte (GB).

random access memory (RAM): the memory in a modern computer system. Access is "random" because the CPU can request anything stored in memory at any time, in whatever order it chooses.

BASIC stands for Beginner's All-Purpose Symbolic Instruction Code. Developed in 1968 by two Dartmouth College mathematicians, John Kemeny and Tom Kurtz, BASIC was designed as a computer language that could be learned easily by novice computer programmers. Updated versions of it are still in wide use today.

punched paper tapes every time the computer was used, and then loading the program the user wanted to run. Wozniak decided to include BASIC inside the computer, so it would be available whenever the machine was switched on. After writing a new version of BASIC in just a few weeks, he included it in the Apple II's read-only memory (ROM), a type of computer memory whose contents were programmed at the factory; they could not be changed, only read. This enabled BASIC to automatically start when the computer did.

To top it all off, the Apple II came fully assembled (except for a monitor). The entire computer was encased in a beige plastic case, with the keyboard built into the top. This was Steve Jobs's idea. As long as the computer worked well, Wozniak would cheerfully have put up with a drab metal box or even exposed wiring. But Jobs knew that for the computer to attract non-hobbyists, it had to look like a well-built, fully packaged product. In addition to being the first minicomputer that could be bought readymade, the Apple II—initially priced around $1,300—was the first the average middle-class person could afford.

THE RESULT

The world got its first look at the Apple II in April 1977 at the West Coast Computer Faire, a hobbyist exposition. Apple Computer rented a large booth near the entrance, where everyone had to pass by. It set up several Apple IIs to run impressive color graphic and sound demonstrations. The booth was a huge success, and within a few months, Apple had received 300 orders for its new computer. By the end of the first year, it had already earned $774,000, with clear profit of $42,000.

"There were about ten things in the Apple II that none of the other computers were going to have for years," Steve Wozniak said later of his invention. "I had put in color, paddles, sound, better language commands, high-density RAMS—a whole environment that went so far beyond just a computer."

Markkula decided that Apple had to up the ante. Like its competitors, the Apple II relied on cassette tapes to store any data the user needed to save. In December 1977, Markkula told Wozniak that Apple needed to show a working floppy disk drive at the next big trade show—in January, only a month away. Collaborating with 17-year-old Randy Wigginton, another Apple employee, Wozniak worked nights, weekends, and even Christmas Day to create and execute a brilliant new design. Thanks to their long hours, the Apple II was the first personal computer to offer a floppy disk drive. Disk storage was faster and more reliable than cassettes, opening the way for more complex, useful Apple II software, such as word processors and databases. It also proved ideal for storing and loading games, one of the computer's big selling points.

The first floppy disks were eight inches in diameter and had small 100K memories. They were thin, flexible disks coated with magnetic material and covered by a protective jacket.

In 1979, a seemingly unrelated event set the Apple II firmly on the road to commercial success: Dan Bricklin and Bob Frankston released the first version of their financial analysis program, VisiCalc. VisiCalc was the first computerized spreadsheet program. Modeled after the paper spreadsheets used by accountants and financial analysts, VisiCalc allowed users to tie rows and columns of data together in ways never before possible. Updating numbers in one cell of VisiCalc's spreadsheet allowed all the others to be recalculated instantly, which made it very useful for "what-if" scenarios. When VisiCalc was released

Bob Frankston (left) and Dan Bricklin, creators of the software program VisiCalc

in 1979, the company sold 500 copies each month, and sales continued to increase at a sharp rate. For the first year, VisiCalc was available only on the Apple II, because that was the only computer the creators had had access to. VisiCalc became the "killer app" (short for application) for the Apple II—it made people want to buy the system just to use that software. Each VisiCalc sale was essentially also an Apple II sale, giving Apple Computer an instant presence in the business world.

The Apple II spawned an entire family of compatible computers, including the Apple II+, the IIe, the IIc, the IIc+, and the IIGS (an enhanced multimedia computer, and the first of the line to offer a modern Graphic User Interface, or GUI). For most of the next decade, the Apple II line was the company's cash cow, funding development of more technically advanced computers such as the Lisa, the Apple III, and most importantly, the Macintosh. The last Apple II model, the Apple IIe, was not discontinued until November 1993.

Apple Computer grew rapidly in the late 1970s and early 1980s, and Wozniak and Jobs became millionaires many times over. Gradually, however, the company's competitors began to catch up. When it became clear that personal computers were more than a passing fad, computer giant IBM decided that it wanted a piece of the action. It sold its first PC in 1981, and within a few years, IBM and IBM-compatible machines dominated the market. Even before Apple began facing problems, however, Wozniak had begun to withdraw from being a major

Graphical User Interface (GUI): the part of a computer program that interacts with the user to show information and receive commands. A GUI (pronounced "gooey") uses pictures or labels, called icons, that represent applications or functions. The user can simply point a device called a mouse on the icon and click to open a file or begin an operation.

player at the company. He loved engineering, but he had no interest in business management. In 1981, after suffering injuries and short-term amnesia when a small plane he was piloting crashed, Wozniak took time off from Apple. Deciding to finish his college degree, he enrolled at the University of California under the name "Rocky Raccoon Clark" (to downplay his famous identity). He finally earned his B.A. in engineering in 1986.

Wozniak did return to Apple in 1983 to work as "just an engineer," and in 1985 he and Steve Jobs received the National Medal of Technology from President Ronald Reagan. Shortly afterward, however, Wozniak realized that working for a large company wasn't what he wanted to do for the rest of his life, and he left Apple for good. Although he continued to be listed as an employee in the Apple corporate database, he spent his days on projects he found more rewarding. He donated money to charities and started several technology companies, the latest of which was Wheels of Zeus (WoZ). Founded in 2001, it developed affordable electronic tags to help keep track of children, pets, and property. An innovative wireless network could monitor these tags and notify customers by phone or e-mail whenever, for instance, their dog left the yard.

In 2000, Steve Wozniak was inducted into the National Inventors Hall of Fame for creating the personal computer and helping to launch a huge industry. But most days, he could be found teaching local fifth-graders how to use computers—Apple computers, of course.

Steve Wozniak divorced his first wife, Alice, in 1980. In 1981, he married Candi Clark, an accountant at Apple. The couple had two sons, Jesse and Stephen Gary Jr., and a daughter, Sara, before divorcing in 1987. Steve found a happier relationship with Suzanne Mulkern, a high-school classmate with three children of her own, and they married in 1990.

When Wozniak graduated from college at age 35, the *San Francisco Chronicle* called him "The Student Most Likely to Already Have Succeeded." Delivering his class' commencement address, Wozniak joked, "I'm glad to have a degree so that now I can go out and get a good-paying job."

CHAPTER SEVEN

Tim Berners-Lee and the World Wide Web

One could say that the Internet was born on October 1, 1969. That day, researchers at the University of California at Los Angeles (UCLA) sent the first message over the Advanced Research Projects Agency computer network (ARPAnet). The message was very simple, just a request to "log in" to a computer at the Stanford Research Institute in Menlo Park, 360 miles to the north. Sponsored by the United States Department of Defense, the network was merely a group of loosely linked computers that used phone lines to communicate with one another. Linked computers could perform tasks more quickly, because they allowed researchers to share data and work together remotely. The operators were able to send the receiving computers instructions instantly, rather than sending magnetic tapes or punch cards through the mail. We take this for granted today, but before the 1960s, it was almost impossible.

Tim Berners-Lee (b. 1955) changed both technology and modern culture when he created the World Wide Web, a system that made the Internet accessible and useful to everyday people.

The creators of ARPAnet pose with their equipment. Front row (left to right): Jim Geisman, Dave Walden, and Will Crowther; back row (left to right): Truitt Thatch, Bill Bartell, Frank Heart, Ben Barker, Marty Thrope, Severo Ornstein, and Bob Kahn.

When it first started running, the ARPAnet linked computers at UCLA, the Stanford Research Institute, the University of California at Santa Barbara, and the University of Utah. By 1972, there were 15 agencies on the network, including the Massachusetts Institute of Technology, Harvard University, and NASA. Eventually the ARPAnet included so many different organizations that it was simply called the Internet. By 1989, connection to the Internet had become almost mandatory for any college or university teaching science, engineering, or technology. Some corporations were also connected, mostly military contractors or companies with whom the researchers worked. But although the Internet was widely used in the research and academic communities, the general public had barely even heard of it. Unless your university or company was on the Internet, you probably didn't know it existed. Practically no one had an Internet connection from home.

The main problem was that the Internet was hard to use. There were many sources of information online, but each type required a different program to access it. E-mail needed a mail program. USENET newsgroups needed a news reader. If you wanted to download a file, you needed a File Transfer Protocol (FTP) program. If your university library's catalog was online, you probably had to use a program called "telnet" to connect to it. Various unconnected systems flourished, with names like Archie, Veronica, Gopher, and WAIS. To make matters worse, there was no such thing as a search engine. In order to find a certain piece of information, you had to know it was out there, know which program to use to access it, and also know exactly where to look for it.

But in 1989, a man named Tim Berners-Lee changed all that. He envisioned a massive, global system for sharing all kinds of databases and making them accessible not with dozens of different programs, but with a single tool. Berners-Lee's tool would allow users to jump from document to document, following links in the text to immediately access more information about whatever they were reading. This kind of document is known as hypertext. Since everything was connected to everything else in Berners-Lee's system, he called it the World Wide Web.

Timothy J. Berners-Lee was born in London on June 8, 1955. His parents had met as part of the team that programmed one of the world's first commercial, general-purpose computers, the Ferranti Mark I. Aside from some bare facts, not much is known about Tim Berners-Lee's childhood or youth. Even when he became very famous, he preferred not to release much information about himself or his family to the public. It is clear, however, that he was fascinated by computers. As a child, he would often "build" them out of cardboard boxes, "running" programs from bits of discarded punched paper tape his parents brought home from work. In the mid-1970s, while studying for a degree in physics at Queen's College, Oxford, he built a real computer using an early microprocessor and an old TV set.

After graduating from Oxford in 1976, Berners-Lee found work as a programmer. In 1980, he began working at CERN (the French acronym for European Organization for Nuclear Research), a large research facility near Geneva, Switzerland. He was an independent contractor helping to develop a new computerized control system for CERN's particle accelerators (machines that allow scientists to study nuclear physics), and his job was daunting. CERN hosted visiting scientists from all over the world who would run their experiments on its equipment, then return to their home universities.

An aerial view of part of CERN's vast facility outside of Geneva

Berners-Lee met many different people each day and had to keep track of their computing needs, research interests, contact information, and relationships to one another. He needed a way to organize all this information so he could make sense of it.

Berners-Lee helped himself keep track by writing a small program called "Enquire." He could type notes into it about people he met, projects he was working on, and anything else he needed to remember. Of course, a simple word processing program would have allowed him to do that, but Enquire also let him create hyperlinks within his documents. For example, if Berners-Lee was writing

Berners-Lee named his program after an old encyclopedia that had fascinated him as a child, *Enquire Within upon Everything.*

hyperlink (or **link**): short for "hypertext link," an embedded reference to a document within another document

about a project and mentioned the name of the person with whom he was working, that person's name could be linked to a document that contained more information about him or her, like a telephone number or directions to an office. Enquire allowed the user to make and follow connections between seemingly unrelated pieces of information, as long as they were all stored on the same computer.

Later that year, Berners-Lee's contract ran out and he left CERN. Since Enquire was created on one of CERN's more obscure types of computers, Berners-Lee didn't bother to keep a copy, and the program was lost. Four years later, however, in 1984, Berners-Lee returned to CERN for a permanent position. His new job involved working with the computers that collected and analyzed the scientific data the accelerators collected. While there, he started to re-create his work on Enquire. Just as before, he used his program to keep track of the connections between the people, projects, and computers he worked with.

It wasn't long, however, before Berners-Lee began to feel the need for a better program. A large organization like CERN produced a lot of different types of documents, from software and hardware manuals for its specialized equipment to technical papers to simple organizational address books. All of this information was on computers, but accessing it required a lot of different programs; research papers, for example, couldn't easily reference information stored in the hardware manuals. It was also difficult to convey data between computers, because CERN employees used many different—often incompatible—types of machines. As Berners-Lee observed, "People brought their machines and customs with them [to CERN], and everyone else just had to do their best to accommodate them. Then teams went back home and, scattered as they were across time zones and languages, still had to collaborate."

To help remedy this situation, Berners-Lee envisioned a system like Enquire, but much more powerful. For one thing, it would be able to make links to information on other computers, something Enquire couldn't do. For another, users would be able to publish their own documents, not just read what Berners-Lee had put in the system. In order to grow and flourish in an often chaotic research network like CERN, the system also had to be decentralized. In other words, there could be no single master database. Individual computers had to manage their own documents, but somehow allow other users on the network to access them easily. Finally, the hyperlinks the system used needed to be able to point to virtually anything, whether it was a word processor document, a program, or an image. A user had to be able to link his or her document to anything else on the network, no matter what type of data it was.

In March 1989, Berners-Lee presented a formal project proposal to CERN's management. In it, he described his vision of the new system, emphasizing the fact that it would make CERN's massive collection of research data and documentation much more accessible to the scientists and technicians who

I would have to create a system with common rules that would be acceptable to everyone. This meant as close as possible to no rules at all.
—Tim Berners-Lee

Berners-Lee's NeXT computer. Introduced in 1988, the NeXT was a sophisticated black cube that used a high-resolution display, a graphical user interface (with windows and menus), and a mouse. Although it was technologically impressive, it was a commercial failure; NeXT stopped producing computers in 1993.

needed it most. Despite his best efforts, though, the proposal languished. It wasn't until the spring of 1990 that Berners-Lee could begin to bring his idea to fruition. CERN had just bought him a new type of computer called a NeXT. It featured some exciting new innovations, and there was a lot of interest in using these computers at CERN. Under the guise of exploring the NeXT's capabilities, Berners-Lee began to work through his ideas. Although at first he tried to find a company whose products he could adapt to his own purpose, he was unsuccessful, and in October 1990 he started writing the first bits of the system he called the World Wide Web.

THE BREAKTHROUGH

Berners-Lee started by designing the program people would use to gain access to his new creation. By the middle of November, he had a working Web client, or browser. At first, it was more like a word processor with hyperlinks than it was like the Internet browsers of today. In addition to reading documents, users could also edit them, and their changes would be available to everyone else. People could use different fonts, set line spacing, and do many other common word-processing tasks.

Next, Berners-Lee had to figure out how to capture all this formatting information and embed it into the documents themselves. If a document's author wanted to have a certain sentence shown in bold type, for example, Berners-Lee had to provide a way for him or her to indicate that in the text. By mid-December, he was working on a solution to this problem, which he called the HyperText Markup Language (HTML). HTML files are simple text files with special tags added to let a web browser know how to format the document properly. For example, the HTML code "Hello, world." would print "Hello, **world**." The "" tag means to turn on bold print, and the "" tag turns it off again. Other tags can specify italics, chapter headings, centered lines and, of course, hyperlinks. By using tags like these, the author of a document can tell the user's browser how to display pieces of the document. It's the browser's job to read the tags and display the document correctly on that particular

Friends at CERN gave me a hard time [about the name World Wide Web], saying it would never take off—especially since it yielded an acronym that was nine syllables long when spoken [double-u, double-u, double-u].
—Tim Berners-Lee

computer system. HTML is very adaptable, which allows the same document to display correctly on both a 19-inch color monitor and a 4-inch monochrome personal digital assistant (PDA) screen.

Just having a browser and a document formatting language wasn't enough. Berners-Lee still needed some way to distribute documents to all of the browsers on the network. To accomplish this, he developed a special program called a Web server. By the end of 1990, Berners-Lee had the world's first Web server, "info.cern.ch," running on his NeXT computer. A browser could contact the server and request a document, and the server would send it. Berners-Lee wrote a simple set of rules governing this interaction between computers—the HyperText Transfer Protocol (HTTP). But he also programmed his browser to follow links to other documents, not just files on HTTP servers. Many popular Internet features, such as news articles and newsgroups, were transmitted by File Transfer Protocol (FTP). Berners-Lee's browser made these available as hypertext pages, thereby adding a huge amount of information to the Web.

Finally, Berners-Lee needed to help a browser find the files posted on a server. In order for the browser to contact a server and ask for a document, it had to know at least three pieces of information: which server to contact, which document to ask for, and what protocol the server used. Berners-Lee put all three bits of information together into one address, which he called a Universal Resource Identifier (URI). A "resource" is usually a document,

protocol: a set of rules that allows computers to interact in a well-defined way. Examples of protocols include File Transfer Protocol (FTP) and Hypertext Transfer Protocol (HTTP).

but it can also be something else, such as a digital photo, a basketball score, or a specific sentence within a document. URIs are now called URLs, or Uniform Resource Locators, and a typical one looks something like this:
http://www.example.com/documents/index.html.

URLs all start by naming the protocol, in this case HTTP. Next, they list the server that has the document, in this case, the computer called www.example.com. Finally, URLs name the file to be retrieved. This example is asking for a Web page called /documents/index.html. Although there are many circumstances where one or more of these pieces can be left out, this is the complete form. This system of URLs helped organize Berners-Lee's Web, allowing diverse types of information to be included and easily located.

By 2001, the World Wide Web had grown so much that CERN needed multiple servers, as well as a staff to administer them.

THE RESULT

What was often difficult for people to understand about the design was that . . . there was no central computer "controlling" the Web, no single network on which these protocols worked, not even an organization anywhere that "ran" the Web. The Web was not a physical "thing" that existed in a certain "place." It was a "space" in which information could exist.
—Tim Berners-Lee

hit: a request for a document on the World Wide Web

In March 1991, after just six months of development, Berners-Lee released the first version of his browser, WorldWideWeb, to some other NeXT users at CERN. There was still only one web server, but it was starting to offer more and more useful local information, so some of the CERN users began to be interested. Because CERN hosted visiting scientists from all over the world, word of Berners-Lee's creation started spreading. Paul Kunz, a physicist from the Stanford Linear Accelerator (SLAC) in California, visited CERN in May to work on the NeXT computers. Kunz was very impressed with Berners-Lee's system, and he brought it back with him when he returned to SLAC a few weeks later. Soon, SLAC was running the first web server outside of CERN.

In August, Berners-Lee packaged up all the web software he had written, including his browser and his web server. He released these on the Internet, making them available for anyone to use. Soon, he began to get e-mail from people who were using his creation. The e-mails usually contained feedback and constructive criticism he used to refine his software and make it more useful. They also informed him of new servers being set up around the world. Every time he heard of a new server, Berners-Lee posted a link from his site to the new one so that people could visit it. During this time, his server on info.cern.ch was receiving 10 to 100 "hits" a day.

By January 1993, there were about 50 known servers, and the Web continued to grow in popularity. As more and more people heard about it, more wanted to use it, and most of them didn't use NeXT computers. Berners-Lee did not have time to create browsers for other computers; he was too focused on keeping the Web going. But he publicly pointed out that creating new browsers would be a useful project for college computing students. Many people followed his suggestion, and there was an explosion of web browsers for all types of computers, some of better quality than others. The web browser whose effects can most clearly be seen today was Mosaic, written by student Marc Andreeson and staff member Eric Bina at the University of Illinois's National Center for Supercomputing Applications (NCSA). After the first test versions were made available in February 1993, Mosaic quickly became the world's most popular browser. It was soon available for many different types of computers, including Apple Macintoshes and IBM-compatible PCs. For years, people didn't just say something was "on the Web," they said it was "on Mosaic."

Andreeson and Bina were quick to add new features to their software to make it do what users wanted and needed. Before Mosaic, for example, most Web pages were just text. Mosaic allowed users to insert images (such as logos or photos) into their pages to make them more interesting. The software also pioneered the use of color in text and in the backgrounds of pages. In mid-1994, with Mosaic's popularity at its peak, Andreeson teamed up with

Jim Clark, a wealthy executive, to develop a new, even better web browser. Their product, Netscape Navigator, dominated the market for quite some time until it lost much of its share to Microsoft's Internet Explorer.

Often available for free on the Internet, such browsers made the Web accessible to virtually anyone with a computer and a telephone line. The Web grew into a major section of the Internet, and the number of Internet users grew at an enormous rate. In 1995, there were an estimated 39,479 all over the world; by the end of 2002, the number had jumped to a staggering 665 million. As always, where there are people, there are businesses, and the Web was no exception. The 1990s will long be remembered as the decade of the "dot-com bubble," in which thousands of new Web-based companies formed and became fabulously wealthy for a short time. When the bubble burst in 2001, most of these new companies went out of business because they had relied on their popularity with Web users to make a profit in the future somehow, rather than using the more traditional (and successful) model of selling useful goods or services.

As the creator of the Web, Berners-Lee surely could have turned his idea to his financial advantage, too. But while others were making millions using the technology he developed, Berners-Lee chose a much more altruistic path. In 1994, he left CERN for the Massachusetts Institute of Technology, where he founded and directed the World Wide Web Consortium (W3C)—a nonprofit

> The arrival of Web software and services as a commercial product was a very important step for the Web. Many people would not really want to use the Web unless they could be sure they could buy the products they needed from a company with all the usual divisions, including customer support.
> —Tim Berners-Lee

organization dedicated to setting new technical standards for the Web and keeping it free for all to use. In 2004, Berners-Lee was knighted in Great Britain for his contribution to technology. His greatest reward, however, was seeing his invention become part of everyday life. Although others modified his original Web, Berners-Lee set the standard for how the Internet would work—and how quickly it could spread. By 2004, nearly half of all Americans relied on the World Wide Web for a myriad of needs, including shopping, research, entertainment, and connecting with other people. Just as the name promised, the World Wide Web is truly a global connection—and it all started in the mind of Tim Berners-Lee.

As director of the W3C, Berners-Lee often spoke at conferences. "People have sometimes asked me whether I am upset that I have not made a lot of money from the Web," he once said. "What is maddening is the terrible notion that a person's value depends on how important and financially successful they are. . . . That suggests disrespect for the researchers across the globe developing ideas for the next leaps in science and technology."

The Next Big Thing

Today's computers are much faster and more powerful than their ancestors. In 1971, the first microprocessor could perform about 60,000 computations a second. Today, a good desktop personal computer can do more than 3 billion. And while we measure electronic computers in operations per second, older mechanical devices, such as Charles Babbage's Analytical Engine, would probably have been measured in seconds per operation.

In 1965, Gordon Moore, one of the founders of the microchip company Intel, made a famous statement. He observed an almost exponential growth in the number of transistors in each generation of integrated circuits, and he foresaw that this growth would continue. In what became known as "Moore's Law," he predicted that the number of transistors on an integrated circuit (such as a microprocessor) would double about every 18 months. Time proved him correct.

The Power Mac G5, introduced by Apple Computers in 2004, offered users four times the memory of a typical personal computer, along with increased speed.

123

Gordon Moore (b. 1929) was one of the first to foresee what the development of integrated circuits meant for the future of computer science.

Moore's Law seems to be widely misinterpreted, though. Many people equate the number of transistors in a CPU with its performance, and therefore they wrongly believe that Moore's Law predicts a doubling of computer performance every 18 months. In theory, that may be true, but the CPU is only part of the total picture of a computer system, and it relies on a number of other components. The computer's memory must supply the necessary values to be computed, which might first need to be read from the hard drive. The system also relies on a motherboard to route the data between the memory chips, the hard drive, and the CPU. All of these components have an effect on the overall speed of the computation.

Consumers are still hungry for computing speed, whether for scientific, engineering, business, or entertainment purposes. So how can engineers overcome hardware limitations inside even the most advanced computers? How can we break through the barrier and reach the next level of computer capability? The answer may lie in changing the way we use computers to solve our problems. Instead of using a single computer, which works through a program serially (from beginning to end), we can break up some types of problems and have many different computers work on pieces at the same time.

For extremely large problems, this parallel processing approach works very well. People can buy professional-grade desktop systems that have two, four, or even eight different CPUs inside. Software written with parallel processing in mind can use several CPUs at once, farming out different pieces of the job. If a single CPU can complete a job in 60 minutes, a four-processor system might complete it in 15 minutes. But there is a practical limit to the number of CPUs you can fit into a computer and still have a usable system. And even with several processors working at once, some problems are just too large to compute in any reasonable amount of time. In 1997, a group of astronomers at the University of California at Berkeley had such a problem.

The astronomers' project was part of an effort called the Search for Extra Terrestrial Intelligence (SETI). They were planning to attach a special receiver to the Arecibo radio telescope in Puerto Rico. While the telescope was being used for normal research, the Berkeley team would digitally record all the radio signals from space across many frequencies, from whatever direction the telescope was pointing. Their hope was to find a recognizable pattern among the random noise produced each day by the universe. But the digital recordings would generate 20 to 35 gigabytes (GB) of raw data each day, and thoroughly checking all this data for patterns involved a tremendous number of calculations. Even with the fastest computers available, the processing would have taken more than a million years. But by 1997, the growth of the Internet had made a new solution possible. This project was a good candidate for a technique known as distributed computing, where a group of computers work together to solve a large problem quickly.

The researchers realized that there were tens of millions of computers connected to the Internet, and almost none of them were constantly busy. In fact, most computers are idle most of the time. Even a fast typist can't generate enough input to keep a computer busy; the computer just spends most of its time waiting for the next keystroke. If the astronomers could "borrow" some of that idle CPU time from some of the millions of computers, they could drastically reduce the amount of time spent combing through their data haystack looking for needles.

On May 17, 1999, the researchers released SETI@home, a special screensaver (a program that displays pleasing "eye candy" on the screen when the computer is idle for a few moments). Instead of just drawing typical geometric patterns or pretty pictures, though, this screensaver contacted the Berkeley servers and downloaded a tiny piece of telescope data. Whenever the screensaver was active, the computer would process the data while showing the user a visually interesting display of the progress of the calculation. When the user needed to use the computer, the screensaver stopped—until the computer went idle again, whereupon it picked up where it left off. When the calculation was finished, the screensaver logged back in to the Berkeley servers, uploaded the processed data, and received a new piece to process. Since many people were interested in finding life on other worlds, the SETI team believed it might be able to get 100,000 users running this software.

By 2003, there were about 4.7 million users of SETI@home. A substantial portion of these people had more than one computer—even many computers—running the software. The project had so far received answers from around 1 billion individual computations, and more than a million more arrived each day. Since its debut in 1997, SETI@home had collected a jaw-dropping 1.6 million years' worth of spare computing time. That's the equivalent of a single computer operating at 57.95 trillion calculations a second! The world's fastest supercomputer, Japan's Earth Simulator, could perform "only" 40 billion calculations per second. By harnessing the massive power of spare CPU time on the Internet, the SETI@home team had built the world's most powerful computing system—and it didn't even have to use its own computers to do it. SETI@home's style of distributed computing was later used for several other large scientific problems, although none was successful on the same scale.

In the SETI@home model, each of the computers involved was entirely separate from all the others. Other than downloading the data and uploading the results, the screensavers didn't communicate with the outside world at all. For some types of problems, this was acceptable, but other problems require a lot of communication between the computers involved. That's why a newer approach, called grid computing, began gaining attention and interest. Like a power grid, where you can simply plug an electrical device in anywhere and expect it to work, a computing grid consists of a

One of the most interesting distributed computing projects was Stanford University's Folding@home, which studied the way proteins assemble themselves within a cell. Stanford scientists hoped to use the information gleaned from their project to further their knowledge of diseases like Bovine Spongiform Encephalitis ("mad cow disease"), Parkinson's, and Alzheimer's.

number of computers and data storage devices that have been made to work together as a logical whole. Yet the grid may consist of thousands of computers from different institutions all over the world. Grid users can write virtually any sort of program they want and access any of the grid's resources. A program running on CPUs in Germany, Switzerland, Canada and the United States could easily access data stored in Italy and display it to a terminal located in Japan. The grid would share not only CPU power, but all the other resources the program needed as well.

In 2005, grid computing was in its infancy, but scientists still used it to compute answers to some really big problems. The European Union established the DataGrid project to explore how its universities and research labs could more easily share their computing resources. The U.S. government had several experimental grids, some of which were to be used for very specific purposes, like the Particle Physics Data Grid (PPDG) funded by the Department of Energy. Commercial products had begun to appear that promised to solve some of the problems associated with grid computing. Although the technology hadn't yet matured, scientists and engineers around the world used it to solve real problems every day.

Distributed computing was not the only avenue forward, though. By 2005, $1,500 desktop computers were often faster than multimillion-dollar supercomputers were just 10 years before. What was a powerful desktop computer in the 1990s seemed more like an amusing toy at the turn of the twenty-first century. A decade later, people might be able to say the same thing again. The Internet and World Wide Web could become "old tech," much as fax machines and photocopiers did in a world of e-mail and instant messaging. We routinely use computers to help design newer, better computers, so it stands to reason that as those newer, better computers become available, they will be used to develop even newer, even better computers. This is a steep upward spiral—the climb of technology. Based on past evidence, there is no reason to expect that its pace will slacken anytime soon.

As part of the DataGrid project, the European Organization for Nuclear Research (known by its French acronym, CERN) in Switzerland joined with technology corporations to create a laboratory for research on grid computing.

abacus: a manual calculating device consisting of parallel rods strung with movable counters

BASIC: Beginner's All-purpose Symbolic Instruction Code, a powerful and easy-to-learn early computer programming language

byte: a unit of computer memory, usually holding a single printed character or small number. A **kilobyte** (**K** or **KB**) equals 1,024 bytes, a **megabyte** (**MB**) equals 1,024 kilobytes, and a **gigabyte** (**GB**) equals 1,024 megabytes.

capacitor: an electronic component that absorbs a charge and releases it into a circuit later, either all at once or more gradually

central processing unit (CPU): the part of a computer that interprets and carries out instructions

chip (or **microchip**)**:** a small piece of semiconductor material on which an integrated circuit or electrical component is created; also used as a term for the integrated circuit itself

circuit: a collection of components through which electricity flows

digital: expressing information in numbers

diode: an electronic component that acts as a one-way gate, keeping electricity flowing in the same direction around the circuit

distributed computing: a way of solving large problems by distributing parts of them among many different computers on a network (such as the Internet)

electromechanical computer: a computer operated by both electricity and moving parts (such as gears, levers, or switches)

electronic computer: a computer operated entirely by electricity

floppy disk: a thin, flexible disk coated with magnetic material and covered by a protective jacket, used to store computer data

germanium: an element that acts as a semiconductor and is used in transistors and integrated circuits

Graphical User Interface (GUI): the part of a computer program that interacts with the user to show information and receive commands. A GUI (pronounced "gooey") uses pictures or labels, called icons, that represent applications or functions. The user can simply point a device called a mouse on the icon and click to open a file or begin an operation.

grid computing: a large-scale effort to build vast networks of computers that can work together to solve problems

hardware: the physical parts of a computer system, such as the CPU, disk drive, memory, keyboard, and monitor

Hertz: a measure of speed in a computer system; each Hertz corresponds to a single operation per second. A **megahertz (MHz)** equals 1,000,000 operations per second, and a **gigahertz (GHz)** equals 1,000,000,000 operations per second.

hit: a request for a document on the World Wide Web

hyperlink (or **link**): short for "hypertext link," an embedded reference to a document within another document

hypertext: a system in which documents are linked to other relevant documents, and readers can follow the links as they desire more information about specific topics

HyperText Markup Language (HTML): a document formatting standard used on the World Wide Web. An author can insert "tags" in a document to show how it should be displayed on a browser.

HyperText Transfer Protocol (HTTP): the method by which servers and browsers agree to exchange documents and files on the World Wide Web

integrated circuit (IC): all the components and interconnections of an electronic circuit integrated onto a single chip. All microprocessors are central processing units on a chip, but not all ICs are CPUs.

Internet: an interconnected system of networks linking computers around the world

killer app: (short for "killer application") a program so popular that people buy computers just to use it

mechanical computer: a computer that relies on the motion of parts such as gears, levers, or switches

microprocessor: a complex, programmable chip that acts as a computer's central processing unit

minicomputer: a mid-sized computer, smaller than a mainframe (a large, powerful computer that often has multiple terminals) but larger than a personal computer

parallel processing: a way of solving large problems by dividing them among multiple CPUs working simultaneously, either within a single computer or in a network of computers

patent: government recognition that an invention belongs to a particular inventor, which gives the inventor the sole right to produce and sell the invention for the duration of the patent

personal computer (PC): a small computer for use by an individual

program: a detailed set of instructions that tells a computer which operations to perform and in what order

proof: a strict, step-by-step demonstration that clearly shows the truth of a mathematical statement

protocol: a set of rules that allows computers to interact in a well-defined way. Examples of protocols include File Transfer Protocol (FTP) and HyperText Transfer Protocol (HTTP).

punch card: a card punched with a pattern of holes representing data to be fed into a computer

random access memory (RAM): the memory in a modern computer system. Access is "random" because the CPU can request anything stored in memory at any time, in whatever order it chooses.

read-only memory (ROM): a type of computer memory whose contents are programmed at the factory; they cannot be changed, only read

resistor: an electronic component that restricts the flow of electricity through a circuit

semiconductor: a class of materials whose ability to conduct electricity lies between that of good insulators (such as rubber) and powerful conductors (such as copper). Semiconductors conduct electricity under certain circumstances, such as when impurities are added to them.

silicon: an element that acts as a semiconductor and is frequently used in integrated circuits

software: the instructions that make a computer do useful things. Operating systems, spreadsheets, e-mail programs, and games are examples of different types of software.

spreadsheet: a piece of paper or computer program with rows and columns for recording data (usually financial data)

transistor: an electronic component, made of semiconductor material, that amplifies electricity within a circuit or turns it rapidly on and off

Uniform Resource Locator (URL): an address used to identify documents on the World Wide Web

vacuum tube: a sealed glass or metal tube with most of the air removed and three electronic components: a cathode (or filament), an anode (or plate), and a grid to channel the flow of electricity between the two. Vacuum tubes amplify electricity or turn it rapidly on and off.

Web browser: a program allowing users to sort through and read information on the World Wide Web

World Wide Web: a section of the Internet made up of servers that use the HTTP protocol and HTML language

BIBLIOGRAPHY

Babbage, Charles. *Passages from the Life of a Philosopher* (1864). Ed. Martin Campbell-Kelly. New Brunswick, N.J.: Rutgers University Press, 1994.

Barker-Plummer, David. "Turing Machines." *The Stanford Encyclopedia of Philosophy*, Winter 2004 Edition. http://plato.stanford.edu/archives/win2004/entries/turingmachine/.

Berners-Lee, Tim, and Mark Fischetti. *Weaving the Web: The Original Design and Ultimate Destiny of the World Wide Web by Its Inventor.* San Francisco: HarperCollins, 1999.

Collier, Bruce, and James MacLachlan. *Charles Babbage and the Engines of Perfection.* New York: Oxford University Press, 1998.

Computer Industry Almanac, Inc. "USA Tops 160M Internet Users." December 16, 2002. www.c-i-a.com/pr1202.htm.

Copeland, Jack. "Biography of Turing." www.alanturing.net/turing_archive/pages/Reference%20Articles/Bio%20of%20Alan%20Turing.html.

Fernandes, Luis. "History of the Abacus." www.ee.ryerson.ca:8080/~elf/abacus/history.html.

Freiberger, Paul, and Michael Swaine. *Fire in the Valley: The Making of the Personal Computer.* New York: McGraw-Hill, 2000.

Goldstine, Herman H. *The Computer: From Pascal to von Neumann.* Princeton, N.J.: Princeton University Press, 1972.

"A History of the Microprocessor." www.intel.com/intel/intelis/museum/online/hist_micro/.

Hodges, Andrew. *Alan Turing: The Enigma.* New York: Simon & Schuster, 1983.

———. http://www.turing.org.uk/.

IEEE Computer Society. "Harry M. Goode Memorial Award." www.computer.org/awards/awdhg.htm.

Keenan, Marty. "Kilby's Accomplishments Traced to a Kansas Blizzard in 1938; A Neighbor's Radio Began His Interest in Electronics." *Great Bend Tribune*, September 19, 2001. http://shorock.com/kilby/article2.html.

Kendall, Martha E. *Steve Wozniak: Inventor of the Apple Computer*. New York: Walker, 1994.

Kilby, Jack. "Jack S. Kilby—Autobiography." www.nobel.se/physics/laureates/2000/kilby-autobio.html.

McCartney, Scott. *ENIAC: The Triumphs and Tragedies of the World's First Computer*. New York: Walker, 1999.

McGrath, Daniel F., Jr. "A Tribute to Dr. J. Presper Eckert." www.luckbealady.com/eckertproject.

The Math Forum at Drexel University. "Ask Dr. Math: History of Numbers." http://mathforum.org/library/drmath/view/52467.html.

Park, Edwards. "The Object at Hand: What a Difference the Difference Engine Made." *Smithsonian*, February 1996. www.smithsonianmag.si.edu/smithsonian/issues96/feb96/object.html.

Pastore, Michael. "Worldwide Internet Users to Pass 500 Million Next Century." www.clickz.com/stats/sectors/geographics/article.php/5911_200001.

The Planetary Society. "SETI@home." www.planetary.org/html/UPDATES/seti/SETI@home/default.html.

Quittner, Joshua. "Tim Berners-Lee." *Time*, March 29, 1999.

Rahimzadeh, Ari. "The Woz Interview!" *The PowerGS*, Issue #5. www.woz.org/pages/wozscape/pgsinterview.html.

Redin, James. "The Calculator and the Birth of the Microprocessor." www.xnumber.com/xnumber/tedhoff.htm.

Reid, T. R. *The Chip: How Two Americans Invented the Microchip and Launched a Revolution.* New York: Simon & Schuster, 1984.

Riddle, John, and Jim Whiting. *Stephen Wozniak and the Story of Apple Computer.* Bear, Del.: Mitchell Lane, 2001.

"Robert Noyce." www.pbs.org/transistor/album1/addlbios/noyce.html.

Rosenbaum, Ron. "Secrets of the Little Blue Box." *Esquire,* October 1971.

Schneiderman, Ron. "Marcian (Ted) Hoff: Teenage Prodigy, Still Going Strong." *Electronic Design,* October 21, 2002. www.elecdesign.com/ (type 2854 in the second search box).

SETI@home. "Current Total Statistics." http://setiathome.berkeley.edu/totals.html.

Slater, Robert. *Portraits in Silicon.* Cambridge, Mass.: MIT Press, 1987.

Sullivan, W. T., et. al. "A New Major SETI Project Based on Project Serendip Data and 100,000 Personal Computers." http://setiathome.ssl.berkeley.edu/woody_paper.html.

Swade, Doron. *The Difference Engine: Charles Babbage and the Quest to Build the First Computer.* New York: Viking, 2000.

Texas Instruments. "About Jack." www.ti.com/corp/docs/kilbyctr/jackstclair.shtml.

von Neumann, John. "First Draft of a Report on the EDVAC." www.wps.com/projects/EDVAC/index.html.

Walker, Rob. "Interview with Marcian (Ted) Hoff." *Silicon Genesis: Oral Histories of Semiconductor Industry Pioneers.* www.stanford.edu/group/mmdd/SiliconValley/SiliconGenesis/TedHoff/Hoff.html.

Weyhrich, Steven. "Apple II History, Chapter 4." www.apple2history.org/history/ah04.html.

INDEX

ABOUT THE AUTHORS

Gina De Angelis is the author of more than 30 books and articles for children and young adults. She holds a bachelor's degree in theater and history, and a master's degree in history. A native of Pennsylvania, Gina has also lived in Australia, Vermont, and Mississippi.

David J. Bianco has been a system administrator for more than a decade. He started his career lurking around his university's computer science lab, forcing the staff to either call security or give him a job. (Fortunately, they gave him a job.) He is currently a freelance technical writer and computer security analyst for a U.S. nuclear physics laboratory.

PHOTO ACKNOWLEDGMENTS

Apple Computer, Inc: pp. 96, 101, 122

Bletchley Park Trust (www.bletchley-park.org.uk): pp. 39, 41

CERN: front cover, pp. 106, 111, 114, 117, 121, 129

Charles Babbage Institute, University of Minnesota: pp. 44, 53, 55, 108

Fairchild Semiconductor International: p. 70

IBM Archives: pp. 50, 88, 102

Intel Corporation: pp. 60 (bottom/right), 76, 79, 82, 84 (both), 86, 87, 89, 124

King's College Library, Cambridge: p. 42 (AMT/K/7/17)

Library of Congress: pp. 6, 18, 57

Lucent Technologies, Bell Laboratories: pp. 63, 64

Alan Luckow: p. 90

National Archives: pp. 10, 11, 12, 49

National Portrait Gallery, London: pp. 16, 30

PhotoDisc: p. 9

Science Museum/Science and Society Picture Library: pp. 24, 26, 27, 29, back cover

Texas Instruments: pp. 60 (top/left), 65, 67, 69, 72, 74, 75

Unisys Corporation: p. 59

Software Arts/Dan Bricklin: p. 103

Steve Wozniak: pp. 94, 97